MW00948018

Interpreting the Rubrics and Prompts
for the PACT

Written By Dr. Gwen Brockman

Edited By Clayton Brockman

2nd Edition

I am grateful for the editing skills of Clayton Brockman and for his patience with me during the process of putting this workbook together. Many thanks and I love you very much.

I would also like to thank Dr. Jeff Sapp for his input on Bilingual Education and to the candidates that have provided sound advice that is printed in this book. Good luck in your teaching careers!

ISBN – 9781530548446

ISBN - 9780615957050

Table of Contents

Page

Overview   1

What is a Teaching Event? Power Point   2

Getting to Know the Materials: Scavenger Hunt   7

The Big Picture   8

Chapter 1   8

Chapter 2   17

Chapter 3   41

Chapter 4   47

Chapter 5   57

References   62

Appendices

Appendix 1 – Learning Segment Sample Template   63

Appendix 2 – Task Validation Sample Template   64

Appendix 3 – CELDT Strategies Sample Template   66

Appendix 4 – Scaffolding Terminology Sample   69

Appendix 5 – Context for Learning Commentary Rubric   71

Appendix 6 – Suggested Rubric Elements for Content Areas   73

Appendix 7 – Checklists for Peer-Review   74

Appendix 8 – Sample Theoretical Frameworks   114

Overview

The teaching event is a mandatory California Teacher Assessment requirement for all multiple and single subject teachers, and its requirements, handbooks, guides, and scoring rubrics are available at the PACT website www.pacttpa.org. All of that can overwhelm any teacher. This guide, then, was designed to help the user to understand the requirements, interpret the rubrics and prompts, connect the sections of the teaching event, and aid writing the assessment. Many of the documents within this guide are taken directly from the PACT website. Because the teaching event is based in content areas, this guide will use "content" as a generic term to refer to any area of study. When specificity is necessary, the guide will indicate the content area by name.

There are five sections to the Teaching Event:

- Context for learning
- Planning
- Instruction
- Assessment
- Reflection

The five sections are interrelated and the user will need to make the necessary connections to complete the Teaching Event. This guide will help the teacher candidate to fulfill and address the sections' requirements both independently and collectively.

What is a Teaching Event?

The Teaching Event (TE) is a summative performance assessment that meets the requirements for a California Teaching Credential. The TE is intended to be a capstone assessment that requires novice teachers to plan a series of integrated lessons, video tape their instruction, analyze student work, and reflect on their teaching.

How do I fulfill this requirement?

- Enroll in the required class
- Choose a 3 to 5 day learning segment
- Video tape one or more of the lessons within the learning segment
- Write a document that includes all of the components required for the Teaching Event
- Submit your Teaching Event on time!

How can I prepare myself to complete this assignment?

- Don't procrastinate! This assignment takes time to video and write.
- Video tape more than one lesson.
- Prepare your learning segment well in advance.
- Use the "buddy system" for editing and accountability for your Teaching Event.
- Most of your courses and assignments are related to the Teaching Event. Look for the components in your coursework.
- Don't procrastinate!

How will my other courses contribute to the Teaching Event?

- The Teaching Event is related to the Teacher Performance Expectations (TPE)
- TPEs are noted in all syllabi for course objectives (including assignments)
- Your Field Evaluations are related to TPEs

_____

_____

_____

_____

_____

_____

What are the components of the Teaching Event?

The TE is divided up into "Tasks"
- Context for Learning (TED 402, 407, 415, 467, 468)
- Planning (TED 400, 402, 407, 411, 467, 468)
- Instruction (TED 407, 411, 466/453, 467, 468)
- Assessment (TED 407, 467 & 468)
- Reflection (TED 467 & 468)
- Academic Language (TED 407, 466/453, 467, 468)

_____

_____

_____

_____

_____

_____

Context for Learning

- Information regarding your student population
  - Academic development
  - Language development
  - Cultural characteristics
  - Social development
  - Socio-economic status
- Classroom resources and characteristics

_____

_____

_____

_____

_____

_____

Planning

- Choose a central focus for your TE (big ideas, content standards, or learning objectives)
- Select grade-level appropriate content standards
- Include students' experiences, interests and prior learning
- Plan "what" and "how" you will assess student learning
- Identify research behind your decisions

_____

_____

_____

_____

_____

_____

Instruction

- Video tape a lesson from the learning segment – up to 20 minutes and two segments
- Tape a lesson that shows yourself teaching to the whole class
- Choices – tape more than one lesson
  - Choose one of the lessons and at most 2 segments

_____

_____

_____

_____

_____

_____

Assessment

- How will you determine student learning?
  - Daily?
  - At the end of your learning segment
- How will you make the curriculum and assessments accessible for ALL of your students?
- What will be your evaluation criteria?
- Gather student samples to turn in with your Teaching Event

_____

_____

_____

_____

_____

_____

Reflection

- How will you address your students as learners?
- Reference research and theories
- How will you determine how well the lessons were taught?

Academic Language

- Should be evident throughout your Teaching Event
- Academic language is subject specific
- Plays a major roll in student learning
- Be aware of the academic language you teach, evaluate, assess, and how your students will acquire it

---

How will my Teaching Event be scored?

- An anonymous scorer who has been previously calibrated and is knowledgeable in your subject area will assign a rubric score for each of your Tasks.
- Your Teaching Event may be read by two or more scorers

General Stuff

- Time management – this is not something that you can "pull an all nighter" and pass
- Read all of the stuff provided for in your Summative Assessment class
- Write your teaching event on-time with the class. Do not write it in retrospect. Students who do this have the tendency to leave out components that should be addressed.
- Video tape early
- Go to the CLASS center for help if you think you may have difficulty writing (TEs are generally 30 to 60 pages)

Questions?

- Your instructor will be able to answer most of your questions

Scavenger Hunt – Getting to know the materials you will need to complete the Teaching Event. In order for you to complete this assignment, you'll need to have a copy of the Teaching Event Handbook and Making Good Choices.

1. On what page and in which document do you find the overview of what to complete and submit for the Teaching Event?

2. Where do I find the information about how to respond to the prompts for the Context for Learning?

3. How will my Teaching Event be scored?

4. Where do you find the daily reflections prompts for the teaching event?

5. What are the guidelines for videotaping your learning segment?

6. What is the recommended number of pages each commentary should total?

7. What is the difference between English learners and students who are proficient English speakers?

8. How many minutes should my video be?

9. What purpose does the "pause for self-assessment" serve?

10. What is Academic Language and where can I find the definition?

11. Is there a specific lesson plan template that I should use?

12. Do I have to put a chart in for the assessment data that is being collected?

The Big Picture

Readings – Teaching Event Handbook pages 1 & 2
Making Good Choices page 1

Completing the Teaching Event can be an overwhelming task. Each semester I get a number of questions regarding what candidates will need to submit, and I always tell them to check on page two of their handbook. This section will also help you get a "big picture" understanding of what you are about to complete. So take the time, read each entry, and don't procrastinate! This is big task and is not an "over-nighter."

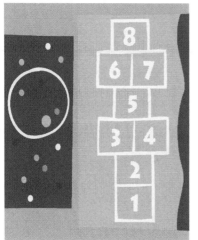

This assessment will measure how well a teacher will be able to scaffold instruction for a specific population; namely your classroom. Let's say that your academically struggling students are at a level 2 (indicated in the picture). Your lesson is at a level 8. Your task will be to scaffold instruction so that ALL of your students can understand a level 8 lesson. The assessment measures both your ability to scaffold for academic discrepancies between students' prior knowledge, the level of the lesson and academic language differences.

Chapter 1

CONTEXT FOR LEARNING

Materials – You will need to go to the PACT website www.pacttpa.org and download the following to use with this book:

- Teaching Event Handbook (in your content area)
- Content area rubrics
- Academic Language (in your content area)
- Making Good Choices
- Selecting a Learning Segment

Readings – Teaching Event Handbook – pgs. 3 – 6
        Making Good Choices page 2

Suggested Instructional Activities (Context for Learning)
- Have the candidates read samples of the Context commentaries, one from a passing teaching event and another from a failing teaching event. Solicit answers from the candidates about the similarities and differences between the two. (I find this activity

important for students to gain the understanding about the level of specificity that is needed to set themselves up to be successful in completing the teaching event.) Also consider having students compare their Context drafts with a passing Context. Included is a rubric that I find helpful for students to gauge their writing in the Context Commentaries (see Appendix 5 for rubric)

- Review the Academic Language Handout.
- In class activity – CEDLT levels and what strategies are associated with each level. (See appendix 3)
- Peer review Context Commentaries

This section provides the necessary information for the assessor to have a documented understanding of what the classroom environment is like and who your student population is. It also provides valuable information that will influence your planning and instructional decisions for your documented learning segment as well as your explanations in each of the commentary areas. Let's take a look at the first series of questions that the Context for Learning will ask.

Context for Learning Section #1

1. How much time is devoted each day to "content" instruction in your classroom?
2. How many students are in the class you are documenting?
3. How many students in the class are English learners?
4. How many students are Redesignated English Learners?
5. How many students in the class are Proficient English speakers?
6. How many students are at the Beginning Listening CELDT level?
7. How many students are at the Early Intermediate Listening CELDT level?
8. How many students are at the Intermediate Listening CELDT level?
9. How many students are at the Early Advanced Listening CELDT level?
10. How many students are at the Advanced Listening CELDT level?
11. How many students are at the Beginning Speaking CELDT level?
12. How many students are at the Early Intermediate Speaking CELDT level?
13. How many students are at the Intermediate Speaking CELDT level?
14. How many students are at the Early Advanced Speaking CELDT level?
15. How many students are at the Advanced Speaking CELDT level?
16. How many students are at the Beginning Reading CELDT level?
17. How many students are at the Early Intermediate Reading CELDT level?
18. How many students are at the Intermediate Reading CELDT level?
19. How many students are at the Early Advanced Reading CELDT level?
20. How many students are at the Advanced Reading CELDT level?
21. How many students are at the Beginning Writing CELDT level?
22. How many students are at the Early Intermediate Writing CELDT level?
23. How many students are at the Intermediate Writing CELDT level?
24. How many students are at the Early Advanced Writing CELDT level?
25. How many students are at the Advanced Writing CELDT level
26. How many students overall are at the Beginning CELDT level?
27. How many students overall are at the Early Intermediate CELDT level?

28. How many students overall are at the Intermediate CELDT level?
29. How many students overall are at the Early Advanced CELDT level?
30. How many students overall are at the Advanced CELDT level?
31. How many students have Individualized Education Plans (IEPs) or 504 plans?
32. How many students participate in a Gifted and Talented Education (GATE) program?

I know you must be thinking, "Wow, this is just the *first* series?" Yes, and they are all important, but manageable, if we can break down the questions for a better understanding of how they will impact your lesson planning and video instruction.

Question #1- "How much time is devoted each day to "content" instruction in your classroom?"

Let's think about this for a minute... Why is this important? The Teacher Performance Assessment requires that you plan for a learning segment that is 3 to 5 lessons; or is between 3 to 5 **HOURS** of instruction; or about a week. So let's say that you teach 45 minutes of your content area a day: That means that you should have at least 4 days of lesson plans, and if you teach 90 minutes a day, then you need a minimum of 2 days of lesson plans... you get the drift. When I talk about your teaching and lesson planning, I want to make it clear that you'll need to "TEACH" something every day; a review or assessment day does not count as a day of instruction. If you feel the need to include a "fun" activity (games, puzzles, videos, etc.) for independent practice for the students, go ahead, but remember that a "fun" day does not count as a day of instruction.

Question #2 - How many students are in the class you are documenting?

The Performance Assessment for California Teachers (PACT) has a minimum requirement of 12 students. You must document each of these students in the Context for Learning and the appropriate commentaries and the assessor should "see" them in your recorded video(s). The recommendation is that you should teach a whole class, but keep in mind that there is a minimum requirement.

Questions #3 & #4 - How many students in the class are English learners? How many students are Redesignated English Learners?

Question #3 is simply asking for the total number of English learners (EL) in your class, but question #4 has some controversy attached to it. According to the California Department of Education, "...Reclassification is the process through which students who have been identified as English learners are reclassified as fluent English proficient (RFEP) when they have demonstrated that they are able to compete effectively with English-speaking peers in mainstream classes." However the Legislative Analyst's Office Report (2006) says "Reclassification Process: English learners are reclassified as 'fluent' when they have sufficient English skills to learn in a regular classroom with extra assistance and perform in academic subjects at approximately 'grade level.'"

The key phrases there are "extra assistance" and "approximately at grade level." Let's deal with the "extra assistance" first. Apparently for those reclassified students, you should consider including appropriate scaffolding or differentiating instruction to support their learning. The areas of support will directly depend upon how you deliver instruction and all associated activities; for example, will you be lecturing to your students? Thus, the oral delivery of the "content" material will need some support to aid in comprehension.

What does "approximately at grade level" mean? Let's think for a moment about your English speaking students; what support do you offer them? Are you including a graphic organizer for them to take notes? Then ask yourself, "Will your EL need 'extra assistance' beyond the graphic organizer?" The Legislative Analyst's Office Report (2006) thinks so. Consider this question: "How do you know if your EL's will need assistance beyond what you originally planned?" At some point in the writing of the Teaching Event you'll need to provide evidence for your EL students in the areas of reading, writing and comprehension; ask yourself the questions now and determine an answer with some certainty before moving forward.

Questions #6 to 30 – There you are identifying where on the CELDT spectrum your students will fall. Those questions are particularly important when planning and delivering instruction. Knowing what your students can and cannot do will greatly impact what strategies you'll use to deliver instruction. Let's look at an example: If you have a student who scores a 1 on the CELDT test, their speaking and listening abilities are primarily in their native language. They may be very capable of higher levels of thinking, but if they can't comprehend what you are saying, they'll have a problem; even worse, you won't know if they lack the "content" understanding or if they have a language issue. Will you be able to lecture to them in English? Should you give them a paper and pencil exam in English? No, of course not! You'll have to do something else to provide the material they'll be learning and to assess their learning. Let's look at the partial table below. I'll discuss this further in the planning section of this guide.

CELDT Level	What students have	What students can do	Strategies Teachers Can Use
1 – Beginning (Beginning English learners can communicate only in their primary language, they are very capable of higher level	• Their primary language • Minimal comprehension of English • Minimal verbal production in English with little or no receptive skills • One/two word responses that	• Nod and shake head to answer questions • Understand simple phrases • Speak a few words to communicate basic needs • Point to objects or print • Sort objects into categories • Pantomime • Draw pictures and label	• Increase vocabulary development through physical movement, realia, drawings, etc. • Provide listening activities e.g., daily listening center with taped picture books • Read aloud predictable and patterned books • Have students label and manipulate pictures and objects.

thinking skills)	may be disconnected or memorized statements	drawings and diagrams • Gesture to show understanding • Match objects or pictures • Give yes/no answers to simple questions • Reproduce what they hear, repeat and recite	• Provide one-on-one time with students

Do you see how the students' level of understanding in English will impact your instructional delivery? If you have students who are CELDT level 1, then your choices of instructional strategies are greatly reduced.

The second important point I'd like to make when answering the language questions is that as the author of the Teaching Event, you are self-identifying subgroups within your classroom. "What does that mean?" It means that within the commentaries of each of the sections within the teaching event, you'll need to address and write to your subgroups. Let's look at an example from the planning commentary prompt:

> *Given the description of students that you provided in Task 1.Context for*
> *Learning, how do your choices of instructional strategies, materials, technology,*
> *and the sequence of learning tasks reflect your students' backgrounds, interests,*
> *and needs? (Teaching Event Handbook – Elementary Mathematics, 2013)*

Does your students' aptitude with English compel you to meticulously choose your instructional strategies, materials, technology, and the sequence of learning tasks? You bet it does! Let's say for a moment that you have EL students who are at the CELDT level 4 and 5. When you have indicated this on the Context for Learning, you will then answer the above prompt by first discussing how your choices of strategies, etc. were affected by your level 4 students and then again for your level 5 students.

Question #31 – Here again, if you have students in your class with either an IEP or a 504 plan, then you will have identified another subgroup within your class. Both of those plans have documented strategies and accommodations that you'll need to incorporate into your planning and instruction. You might consider looking at those documents (the latest versions) and incorporating the necessary accommodations and instructional strategies into your Teaching Event commentaries and lesson plans. You'll also need to know what they can and cannot do in the "content" area.

Question #32 – While most GATE students do not have an IEP, there may be some documentation for their academic learning. If not, then you have identified another subgroup.

Let's look at an accumulative example, let's say that you have CELDT level 4 and 5, IEP, and gate students in your class. You have identified four different subgroups within your room that you will eventually write about, disaggregate their assessment data, and consider when planning for instruction. We'll discuss the academic subgroups in the next section.

Context for Learning Section #2

In this section you will provide an essay that documents the academic, language, and social development of your class as well as the family and community contexts of your students. Let's take each of those individually and discuss how they will affect your planning and instructional delivery.

Academic Development – "Consider students' prior knowledge, key skills, developmental levels and other special educational needs. (TPE 8)" (Teaching Event Handbook – Elementary Mathematics, 2013). You are being asked to describe what the students can and cannot do. In this section, I'd like you to think about who your students are on a learning level as it relates to their academic development in the "content" area. Do you have struggling learners? Do you have students who have "major" holes in their learning in your "content" area? Where are the "holes" in their "content" learning? E.g., it is not uncommon to have students who may have poor estimating or fractional calculation skills but can perform higher levels of math. While it is not impossible to teach those students new content, they do present a challenge when planning for instruction; and you probably have to do some reviewing or remediation before presenting your learning segment that you are documenting for your Teaching Event. (If you can't readily answer those questions, then it appears that a pre-test of skills are in order…)

Consider for a moment how you would identify your class as academic learners. How would you "break" up your class? Let me give you an example – I can break my class down into thirds: one third are struggling learners, one-third are okay with a couple of "holes" in their calculation skills and the last third really don't need any special support. After the identification or categorization, you will need to describe for each of the academic groupings what the students can and cannot do in relation to your "content" area. Using the example above I might describe the "struggling" learners in this way: "My struggling learners often have difficulty remembering how to find common denominators when adding and subtracting fractions. They also do not have their multiplication facts by rote, and they suffer from poor self-efficacy in the area of mathematics. Nearly 80% of the struggling learners in the class I am documenting are English Language learners who have CELDT scores of 4… However, that group of students can adeptly add multiple digit numbers, etc."

Language Development – "Consider aspects of language proficiency in relation to the oral and written English required to participate in classroom learning and assessment tasks. Describe the range in vocabulary and levels of complexity of language use within your entire class. When describing the proficiency of your English learners, describe what your English learners can and cannot yet do in relation to the language demands of tasks in the learning segment. (TPEs 7, 8)" (Teaching Event Handbook – Elementary Mathematics, 2013).

When dealing with this section, you'll need to go back to the first section of the Context for Learning. If you had CELDT level 4 students, then you'll have to discuss what these students can and cannot do with respect to the learning segment you are about to teach, and the same would apply with the CELDT level 5 students as well as your special education students. Let's look at an example: let's say you are about to teach a math unit on adding amounts of money. What skills are the students expected to know? If I were to list the skills as money conversion, counting coins, and finding multiple ways to represent the same amount, I'd have to incorporate vocabulary such as conversion, equality, names of the coins, etc. How would each of the CELDT level and academic levels perform in the area of oral language comprehension? Also, will you be asking your students to write anything or read anything? What are their written language skills like? There's a lot to consider there, and the more information you can provide the better. You do not want an assessor to assume you have students with a wider range of skill abilities or lack of abilities.

On a summative note, let's look at the subgroups that I have identified in the above examples. I have CELDT level 4 and 5, some special education students, some GATE students, and some struggling learners. I have essentially identified five subgroups within my classroom. Because of that, I'll have to plan for and write about each of the groups in my lesson plans and commentaries. At this point, I tell my students to list their categorized subgroups, like this -

1. CELDT 4
2. CELDT 5
3. Special Ed
4. GATE students
5. Struggling learners

- and copy and paste that list into all of the prompts in all of the planning, instruction, assessment, lesson plans and reflection commentaries. It may be appropriate in all of the sections, but it will be in MOST of the prompts. If it isn't appropriate, then it's worth discarding, but if it is relevant, then discuss it according to the prompt. We'll do more of this later.

Mathematical Dispositions – "Consider student attitudes, curiosity, flexibility and persistence in mathematics" (Teaching Event Handbook – Elementary Mathematics, 2013).

Interestingly, students think about their abilities in Mathematics, and what they think does matter. Unlike other content areas, students' beliefs about their "math skills" can adversely affect their abilities to perform; weird huh? In fact, think about your own experiences with math! If you liked it, then chances are you did reasonably well at it. On the other hand, if you despised it, then you might even have experienced physical manifestations such as sweaty palms, increased heartbeat and anxiety from having to take a math test. Students are no different.

According to Pintrich and Schunk (2002), task-related emotions are important when a student engages in learning tasks. There are three emotions that are tied to engagement in learning tasks: 1) process related, 2) prospective, and 3) retrospective emotions. Within each of the three emotions both positive and negative outcomes can be generated.

Process related emotion refers to the emotions that are experienced when a person is actually engaged in the task. Process related emotions include enjoyment and boredom. On the other hand, prospective emotions are related to emotions when one approaches or thinks about engaging in a task. One might experience emotions such as joy or anxiety, though they come into play post-task. Positive retrospective emotions include relief or pride, while negative emotions include sadness, disappointment or shame. When students assign a positive emotion to a task, such as enjoyment, pride or hope, these affective or emotional responses will serve to determine the motivational engagement associated with the task. Negative emotions such as boredom, anxiety or shame will detract from a students' motivational engagement.

McLead (1993) posits that the critical age for development of mathematics self-efficacy beliefs and affect is between the ages of nine and eleven. He also believes that once negative attitudes (distress, avoidance of mathematics, and interference with thinking and memory processes) toward mathematics have been established, it is difficult to change and may persist into adulthood." (Brockman, 2006)

Ask yourself the following question: How do my students feel about their prospective, process and retrospective emotions when approaching Mathematics? If you don't know, then ask them. Duh!

Social Development – "Consider factors such as the students' ability and experience in expressing themselves in constructive ways, negotiating and solving problems, and getting along with others. (TPE 8)" (Teaching Event Handbook – Elementary Mathematics, 2013).

Let's look at your classroom population from a social standpoint. Do your students readily ask questions in class? Do they have difficulty expressing themselves in class? How do they get along with the other students? These questions are important for the assessor to understand the social situation in the classroom. Let's suppose that you will be implementing cooperative learning or think-pair-share. If students are reluctant to participate and they dislike doing group work, then these learning strategies might not be the best choice for your students - DUH! If you like to deliver instruction in a seminar style way, then your students will need to participate in class discussions for you to be able to check for their understanding. I'd like to go back for a moment and give you an example of one of my pet peeves. A candidate reports that students are reluctant to ask questions in class - and *then* he goes on to ask students (in the video) if they have any questions. No one raises their hands and the candidate moves on to the next topic. What was the candidate thinking? If you already know your students don't ask questions, how can you use this mode of questioning to monitor for understanding? Get a grip! You need to find another way to check for understanding.

Family and community contexts – "Consider key factors such as cultural context, knowledge acquired outside of school, socio-economic background, access to technology and home/community resources." (Teaching Event Handbook – Elementary Mathematics, 2013).

This section is important for the assessor to understand how the family and community dynamics affect student learning. Will you be able to assign an internet homework assignment? Do they have access in the home to complete it? If not, are there computers available at the local library? Is there a local library? Along those same lines, are your students expected to help out in the home after school? Do they have somewhere to complete the homework?

This section will also describe your ability to use examples in the class, so carefully reflect on the models and aids that you provide: If I were to teach a unit on the seasons, what examples might I be able to include or how would I describe snow to students who had not had the experience? What about the desert? You might be from Chicago and the cold, windy, and snowy days are very familiar to you, but what about a kid who grew up in Hawaii? When building upon prior knowledge to engage them in constructivist learning, students will need to have some experience or prior knowledge of the examples you'll use in your lesson plans. The point here is to be careful of the examples you use in your lesson plans. If the students are unfamiliar with them, then what's the point? Here's something from my experiences: a student used the vast plains in Kansas as an example of a geometric plane and how the plains in Kansas seemed to go on and on - how many of the intercity urban kids you know have had the opportunities to tour the plains in Kansas?

Section 3 District Requirements and Expectations

"Describe any district, school, or cooperating teacher requirements or expectations that might impact your planning or delivery of instruction, such as required curricula, pacing, use of specific instructional strategies, or standardized tests." (Teaching Event Handbook – Elementary Mathematics, 2013). This section will help you out if the district you are teaching in has put some limitations on what you can teach and how it needs to be taught. If the district you are teaching in uses a pacing plan or pre-set curriculum, let the assessor know; it will be to your benefit.

CHAPTER 2

PLANNING INSTRUCTION AND ASSESSMENT

Readings
- Teaching Event Handbook – pgs. 7 – 10
- Making Good Choices pgs. 3 – 7
- Academic Language Handout
- Selecting a Learning Segment Handout

Suggested Instructional Activities
- 1) Solicit students to come up with a list of scaffolding strategies on the board for both academic and language support; 2) make another list of developmental, motivational and language frameworks that students might need to complete the teaching event; 3) pass out some textbooks that students have used in prior classes or have some students bring in their books (generally five to six) that are relative to the work they will need to complete the teaching event; and 4) watch teaching videos (I get them from YouTube or other internet sources) and have students identify scaffolding support strategies, camera angles, how best to "hear" all of the students, etc. While some are watching the videos, the 5 to 6 students with books will find a quote from the textbook (and from the list on the board) and write it down on a sheet of paper. After they have written one quote, I have the students pass the book (and the paper) on to another student, and so on. It is the goal of this part of the class to get students to write at least two quotes during video watching. After the books have made the "rounds," I take their quotes, scan them and send them copies.
- Peer-review the Planning Commentaries and lesson plans. Included in the appendices are checklists for each of the commentary sections. These checklists are written to the rubrics. There is no direct numerical correlation between rubrics and prompts, i.e., rubric 1 does not align with prompt 1. (see Appendix 7)

The Teaching Event Handbook describes this section as:
> "The Planning Instruction & Assessment task describes and explains your plans for the learning segment. It demonstrates your ability to organize curriculum, instruction and assessment to help your students meet the standards for the curriculum content and to develop academic language related to that content. It provides evidence of your ability to select, adapt, or design learning tasks and materials that offer your students equitable access to mathematics curriculum content." (Teaching Event Handbook – Elementary Mathematics, 2013).

Let's face it, you have a big task ahead in completing the Teaching Event and you're going to need to get organized. The learning segment will need to be 3 to 5 lessons or 3 to 5 hours of instruction and you've identified a number of subgroups within your Context for Learning. Let's look at a generic unit plan template (figure 2.2) and the rubrics that will be used to score your planning section of the Teaching Event. There are three rubrics for the planning section of the

Teaching Event. A "2" is the minimum passing score, so for the sake of this guide, I'll address the level "3" in most areas.

I've taken the Level 3 from the three rubrics in the planning section of the Elementary Math Teaching Event (as an example) and compiled them into the table below (Elementary Math Rubrics, 2013) (figure 2.1); we'll deal with the Academic Language and Assessment rubrics in a moment...

Figure 2.1

EM 1: Establishing a balanced instructional focus. How do the plans support students' development of conceptual understanding, computational/procedural fluency, and mathematical reasoning skills? (TPE 1,4,9)	EM 2: Making content accessible. How do the plans make the curriculum accessible to the students in the class? (TPE 1,4,5,6,7,8,9)	EM 3: Designing assessments. What opportunities do students have to demonstrate their understanding of the standards/objectives? (TPE 1,5,11)
• Learning tasks *or the set of assessment tasks* focus on multiple dimensions of mathematics learning through **clear connections** among computations/procedures, concepts, and reasoning/problem solving strategies. • A **progression** of learning tasks and assessments is planned to build understanding of the central focus of the learning segment.	• Plans draw on students' prior learning **as well as** experiential backgrounds or interests to help students reach the learning segment's standards/objectives. • Plans for learning tasks include **scaffolding or other structured forms of support**[1] to provide **access to grade-level** standards/objectives.	• Opportunities are provided for students to learn what is assessed. • The assessments allow students to show **some depth of understanding or skill** with respect to the standards/objectives. • The assessments **access both productive (speaking/writing) and receptive (listening/reading) modalities** to monitor student understanding.

The intention here is to provide a basic "skeletal" outline for what you'll need to include in your lesson plans. You'll determine your specific content later, but you'll have the necessary things you'll need to incorporate into your lessons. For the other content areas, the strategy remains the same: Look at the rubrics, determine the components or elements you'll need to include, and then insert the content into the lesson plans. We'll take the rubrics one at a time and discuss them individually.

> **"EM 1and M 1**: Learning tasks *or the set of assessment tasks* focus on multiple dimensions of mathematics learning through **clear connections** among computations/procedures, concepts, and reasoning/problem solving strategies." (Elementary Math Rubrics, 2013).

---

[1] Such as multiple ways of representing content; modeling problem solving strategies; relating pictures/diagrams/graphs and equations.

Let's break that into the components that need to be included in the lesson plans. From the rubric above, we can see the need for conceptual understanding, procedural understanding and math reasoning and these are all connected by the learning and assessment tasks.

Now, ask yourself "when and where in the lesson plan should conceptual understanding be taught?" In most cases (mathematically speaking), conceptual understanding will come at the beginning of a new concept (that's the *when*). Where should it be taught (that's the *where*)? Realistically it can be taught in either the engagement or the instructional sequence. So, let's go to the unit plan template and insert it (figure 2.2.) Can it be taught on other days? Sure, but all we're doing right now is outlining a generic plan, penciling in the components so they are not forgotten and then you can fine tune your lesson plan later.

You'll also need to incorporate procedural understanding into the unit plan. Generally, after the students have learned about the new concept, then we teach them the procedure for getting the answers. Ok, when and where should procedural understanding be taught? Let's pencil in a couple of places where it is most likely to occur (figure 2.2).

Lastly we need to incorporate mathematical reasoning. That component is generally taught when the students have the necessary skills (conceptual and procedural understanding) and can apply what they have learned in other examples. It can also be taught daily depending on the intentions of the teacher and how the curriculum is driven. Let's say I'm teaching students to sort shapes by attribute (triangle, square, and rectangle). I've taught the conceptual and procedural understanding, and now I want them to generalize what they have learned to sort the same stack of shapes, but with the addition of multiple sizes and colors of the same shapes. After sorting the shapes, they will need to tell me how they sorted the shapes, why they segregated the new shapes and how they are different (by attribute). Since there are multiple places to incorporate that concept, I'll include them in a couple of likely places on the unit plan template; remember, we are just penciling them in so as to fine tune the lesson plan later.

Since the incorporation of conceptual, procedural and reasoning components are included, the pieces that remain are the "clear connections" of the learning or assessment tasks. You'll have to keep that in mind when you put in your content standards. I teach my students that once their lesson plans are completed, they should make an understandable list of the tasks they incorporated and see if they (and a "study buddy") can identify the progression of learning.

Now that we have dealt with the learning tasks, the rubric indicates that the assessment tasks focus on multiple dimensions; guess what those multiple dimensions might be? You got it! Conceptual knowledge, procedural knowledge, and math reasoning assessment tasks will also need to be connected to each other. As your lessons unfold, you'll need to include samples of your assessment tasks and of course you'll check them for "clear connections" and include conceptual, procedural and math reasoning problems. Let's put those items into the generic lesson plan as a reminder to include them (see figure 2.2 below and Appendix 1 for blank template.) If you choose to use a summative assessment, then you can easily include all three elements (conceptual, procedural, and reasoning). If you choose to use a formative assessment, then this task is a bit more difficult, but definitely doable.

One last thing. In the assessment section, you will need to describe students' prior knowledge. Should you plan for and include a pre-test? What do you think? How will you know what their prior knowledge is if you don't? Can you use prior content area unit tests to retrieve that information? Will those unit tests give you an accurate idea of what the prior knowledge is of your students? Should you have a rubric for this pretest? Let me then ask you, how will you know how well they did if you don't have one? Along the same lines, students will ask me if I think it's a good idea to have the same pretest and posttest for the students. My answer is generally "would you like it and would it be fair if I gave you the final exam on the first day of class when I already knew you may not be able to pass?" No one likes to look like an idiot, even if the test isn't graded.

> **Science 1**: "Learning tasks *or the set of assessment tasks* focus on multiple dimensions of science learning through **clear connections** among science concepts, real world phenomena, and investigation/ experimentation skills." (Science Rubrics, 2014)

Let's break this down and determine where in the lesson plans you will like find each of the components that will need to be incorporated. So ask yourself, where would I teach science concepts? Using the same template as Math's (appendix 1), pencil in where you will likely find science concepts taught. What about connecting what the students are learning to "Real World Phenomena?" And lastly, investigation/experimentation skills; think for a moment: If you are to incorporate all three of these things, what would the lesson plans look like?

For Science many candidates will teach with the 5E learning cycle model: Engage, Explore, Explain, Elaborate, and Evaluate. This type of lesson is not a lecture-based instruction, but rather an active-engagement-inquiry-approach type of lesson. During the Engagement section, the teacher uses an object, event, or question to begin the learning process. That will facilitate connections between what the students know and what they can do. Based on that, does it seem reasonable that the introduction of a science concept might occur during this time?

The Exploration section of this learning cycle is where the object/phenomena are explored. The teacher will help the students to organize their thoughts through questioning, suggesting, providing feedback and guidance, and assess their students' understanding and thought processes.

Of course the investigation/experimentation skills occur during the lab. With that said, do you think you'll need to record a lab for your teaching event?

> **Rubric 2:** Let's look at the first bullet point; "Plans draw on students' prior learning **as well as** experiential backgrounds or interests to help students reach the learning segment's standards/objectives." (Elementary Math Rubrics, 2013)

Again, let's determine the where and when of those items that are most likely to occur. Teachers often use examples that students are familiar with so that they can relate their experiential knowledge to what they are about to learn. That is not only good teaching, but in terms of learning theory, it's the way to go! OK, let's determine the where and when for prior learning. It makes sense that we use prior learning to "trigger" a relationship to something we are about to teach. If I were to teach students about tigers, I might begin by saying "who has seen a cat or has a cat as a pet?" I want the students to begin thinking about what a cat looks like, e.g. long tail, four legs, furry, etc., and then I'll teach them about a tiger. The "where" prior learning occurs will likely occur at least at the beginning of the lesson and the "when" will likely be nearly every day. The where and when are not limited to the example above. Those items can be readily inserted throughout the engagement and instruction sections of your lessons. But for the sake of our skeletal outline, put it somewhere that makes sense to you so that you won't forget to include it!

Next is experiential backgrounds or interests; those are along the same lines as prior knowledge. We might give examples to students so that they have an idea of what is about to come. If I'm teaching students about division with remainders, then I might ask students "have you ever had to share a bag of cookies with other people? How can I be sure that everyone will get the same number of cookies to share them fairly? What happens when we can't divide them equally?" Cookies and sharing may appeal to both experiential background and interests of the students. I know that it appeals to MY interests... Now the question, where and when? That will fall along the same path as prior knowledge. It may indeed occur in other places, but for now we are just penciling in the most likely places. (See lesson template)

> **Rubric 2**: (Second bullet) Plans for learning tasks include **scaffolding or other structured forms of support**[2] to provide **access to grade-level** standards/objectives. (Elementary Math Rubrics, 2013)

The second bullet requires the author to incorporate scaffolding or other means of support so that our previously identified subgroups will have access to the curriculum. We've already added our subgroups to the unit template, but it might be a good idea to add the words "scaffolding/support" as a reminder...

> **Rubric 3:** Opportunities are provided for students to learn what is assessed. The assessments allow students to show **some depth of understanding or skill** with respect to the standards/objectives. The assessments **access both productive (speaking/writing) and receptive (listening/reading) modalities** to monitor student understanding. (Elementary Math Rubrics, 2013)

That level 3 rubric has three components. The first is asking if you have provided students with opportunities to learn what is being assessed. In my experience, credential candidates who miss

---

[2]   Such as multiple ways of representing content; modeling problem solving strategies; relating pictures/diagrams/graphs and equations.

that one are letting the activities they think are "cool" drive the lesson. I think penciling in a reminder might be helpful, and certainly ask your "study buddy" what they think is good practice.

The second bullet point asks the assessor to rate the depth of understanding or skill that you will teach to the students. This may sound a bit vague, but you will want your students to communicate to you what they understand about the curriculum you just taught; and I don't mean that they answered 9 out of 10 multiplication facts correctly. Let me provide an example; you have just taught a lesson on basic multiplication and you ask the students what they have learned today in math. You get one student to say "I learned that 2 times 2 is equal to four" and you have another student say "I learned that multiplication is repeated addition, and if I can add numbers, then I can multiply." Which answer shows "the depth of understanding?" Get it? On another note, what does the first answer measure? Is it conceptual, procedural or math reasoning knowledge? What about the second answer? I want you to keep that in mind so that when you are incorporating formative assessments/monitoring for instruction, you ask the appropriate questions for assessing conceptual, procedural and math reasoning knowledge. You'll have to manipulate your lessons to include some sort of assessment (written or oral) that will show that depth of understanding.

The third bullet point asks you to access both productive and receptive modalities in assessment. This means that at some point during each of the lessons you are either assessing your students through speaking/writing **and** listening/reading. We're not talking about calling on one or two students during the lesson, we are talking about getting a real understanding about how the **whole** class is doing with respect to the lesson you are teaching. In many ways I think the second and third bullet points from figure 2.1 can be put together into one concept, i.e. asking questions. At some point you might consider asking students questions during the lesson that will require them to answer in multiple word responses; I'm not talking about one word utterances such as "add" or "subtract next". Go back to the previous example: How can you get your students to provide you with an answer that shows their understanding like the "I learned that multiplication is repeated addition, and if I can add numbers, then I can multiply"? Let's pencil in the receptive and productive assessments. Where are they located on a lesson plan? Hopefully you'll say throughout instruction, and I'd cheer, "Yippee!" And then I'll ask when should this type of assessment occur? And you'd say throughout the lesson. You don't have to put this type of assessment "everywhere" but it should be regularly visible. I'd like you to think about how often an assessment of this type would need to appear so that you, the teacher, have an idea of what ALL the students understood.

Figure 2.2

Day 1	Day 2	Day 3
Standard 1.1	Standard 1.2	Standard 1.3
Objective 1.1	Objective 1.2	Objective 1.3
Engagement *Prior knowledge* *Experiential or interests* *Receptive/productive*	Engagement *Prior knowledge* *Experiential or interests* *Receptive/productive*	Engagement *Prior knowledge* *Experiential or interests* *Receptive/productive*
Instruction *Conceptual understanding* *Procedural understanding?* *Struggling learners* *Special Ed* *Gate* *CELDT 4* *CELDT 5* *Scaffolding for subgroups* *Receptive/productive*	Instruction *Procedural understanding* *Math reasoning* *Struggling learners* *Special Ed* *Gate* *CELDT 4* *CELDT 5* *Scaffolding for subgroups* *Receptive/productive*	Instruction *Procedural understanding* *Math reasoning* *Struggling learners* *Special Ed* *Gate* *CELDT 4* *CELDT 5* *Scaffolding for subgroups* *Receptive/productive*
Application/Independent *Receptive/productive*	Application/Independent *Receptive/productive*	Application/Independent *Receptive/productive*
Assessment *Clearly connect conceptual, procedural, and reasoning* *Did I assess what I just taught?* *Receptive/productive*	Assessment *Clearly connect procedural and reasoning* *Did I assess what I just taught?* *Receptive/productive*	Assessment *Clearly connect conceptual, procedural, and reasoning* *Did I assess what I just taught?* *Receptive/productive*
Materials	Materials	Materials

We have included the three planning rubrics into our draft template (figure 2.2). We now need to take a look at the Instruction rubrics to ensure that those are covered as well (we'll deal with the Assessment and Academic Language rubrics later.)

Instruction Rubrics - It's important to remember that you will need to video tape yourself teaching a lesson. More importantly, during the planning stage you'll only have 15 to 20 minutes to so (see figure 2.3). The Teaching Event requires you to have one or two unedited clips (except in Art) to show the assessor how fabulous you are. That is not a lot of time to strut your stuff, and you'll need to be very strategic about how you'll plan your lessons. In many cases, I've had students tell me that they are doing very well in their final fieldworks/student teaching and they think that it will be a "breeze" to shoot the video.

WRONG!

Fieldwork supervisors spend multiple hours observing you before making their final assessment. Most of you have 15 to 20 minutes; PERIOD! Another key word to remember is "unedited." You won't be able to record 4 minutes here and 4 minutes there for a total of 20 minutes.

Planning for the Instruction Rubrics

Rubric 4

In the table below (figure 2.3) I've included the two Instruction (Elementary Math) rubrics at the "3" level (Elementary Math Rubrics, 2013).

The reason we are dealing with these rubrics now is that you'll want to maximize your opportunities for video clips that will not only show how wonderful your teaching is, but also to provide which sections of your video will meet the demands of the instruction rubrics.

Figure 2.3

EM4: Instruction – Engaging Students in Learning. How does the candidate actively engage students in their own understanding of mathematical concepts and discourse?	EM5: Instruction – Monitoring Student Learning During Instruction. How does the candidate monitor student learning during instruction and respond to student questions, comments, and needs?
• Strategies for intellectual engagement seen in the clip(s) offer **structured opportunities** for students to **actively develop** their own understanding of mathematical concepts and discourse. • These strategies reflect **attention to student characteristics, learning needs, and/or language needs**.	• The candidate monitors student understanding by eliciting student responses that require mathematical reasoning or problem solving strategies. • Candidate responses **build on student input to guide improvement** of students' understanding of mathematical concepts and discourse.

Let's look at each of the bulleted items individually. For EM4 the first bullet reads:

> "Strategies for intellectual engagement seen in the clip(s) offer structured opportunities for students to actively develop their own understanding of mathematical concepts and discourse." (Elementary Math Rubrics, 2013)

What does "structured opportunities for students to actively develop their own understanding of mathematical concepts and discourse" mean? Let's break this down into two sections. According to folks at PACT and many others as well, there is a distinct difference between intellectual engagement and participation. According to Dictionary.com, an intellectual is defined as "A person who engages in academic study or critical evaluation of ideas and issues." As an assessor, I am looking for the teacher candidate that will encourage their students both to engage critically with topics on a conceptual level and to generalize the ideas into new applications/situations and can speak critically about issues related to the topic. What it doesn't mean is that the students are sitting down, shutting up and looking at the teacher.

The other part of the statement tells us that the folks at PACT are looking for discourse. Does that mean students are providing one word utterances such as "4" or "Alaska?" NO! According to Merriam-Webster, discourse is defined as "a mode of organizing knowledge, ideas, or experience that is rooted in language and its concrete contexts, is formal and orderly and usually extended expression of thought on a subject (larger than a sentence)." Let's put it all together: intellectual engagement is when students are actively talking about the concept you are teaching, can critically evaluate the ideas and issues related to your topic, and are speaking in lengths greater than a sentence.

Now that we have those parts defined, they will need to be included in your video. So, somewhere within your 15 to 20 minutes of instruction I should "see" and "hear" the students "engaging intellectually through discourse" at least once. Going back to our original outline of the learning segment, where and when can we put this intellectual engagement? Take a look at figure 2.5 below and ask yourself, where and when is a good place for intellectual engagement and discourse?

It would seem that we already have opportunities for this type of engagement within the learning segment template… How about the "receptive/productive" piece? Can you include questioning that will encourage students to engage intellectually with the content? You bet! But where?

 Anywhere! But remember that you will need to include it in your video. So let's break it down a bit more. The engagement or introduction section of the lesson is used to tap into students' prior knowledge and to motivate them to learn more about the wonders of the world through your lessons. Does this sound like the perfect place for this type of discourse? How about during instruction where you are teaching them about something new? That is a likely place, and we already have the receptive/productive notation on the template. I'd like you to clarify this notation a bit more (added an ID) and put a * in front of it. The * will indicate that this is where the learning segment meets the needs of the instruction and planning rubrics (see figure 2.5).

How about the application or independent practice section of the lesson plan? Is that a good place to include the "intellectual engagement of conceptual knowledge?" In fact, it is not only a good place, but it also provides an opportunity for you to assess your student learning; double the benefits!

In the independent practice section, you have a couple of options. You can ask questions for the students to respond orally, or you can also get them to write about what they have learned. Remember that productive language is not only spoken but can be written as well. One word of caution here, though: the writing prompt will need to encourage students to write about their understanding through engagement with the content and critically examine the issues or ideas related to your topic.

The next bulleted item reads: "These strategies reflect **attention to student characteristics, learning needs, and/or language needs**." (Elementary Math Rubrics, 2013) How do we pay attention to student characteristics, learning needs and/or language needs? If we go back to the Context for Learning, didn't you describe student characteristics as they apply to their academic, learning, language, social and familial contexts? You bet! Did you copy and paste your subgroup lists into/onto your lesson plans and commentaries? If you haven't, get to it now. Since you self-identified your subgroups and I asked you to cut and paste your list into each of the commentary sections and into the lesson plan, we are in good shape to move forward. Excellent pedagogy relies on scaffolding or differentiating instruction to meet the needs of our student populations. If you look at the template in the instruction section (see figure 2.5), put a * by the subgroups you have identified. Remember, the * means it's a good part of the lesson to include in the video.

> Science 4: Strategies for intellectual engagement seen in the clips offer **structured opportunities** for students to **actively** collect, analyze, and interpret scientific data. **No potential safety problems** are visible in the videotapes. (Science Rubrics, 2015)

The other components to this rubric are the same as are seen in the Mathematics example provided previously. However, we have to address the differences; namely, the need for students to **actively** collect, analyze, and interpret scientific data. What does that mean to you? It appears that you will need to provide a video of a lab. Not only that, but for this hypothetical lab, we will need to see the students collect, analyze and interpret the data. Remember that as you lesson plan, you will have the opportunity to present two unedited clips. But to show students collecting, analyzing and interpreting data on camera will be a bit of a challenge to you. Ask yourself: Will I need to change the way my lessons are normally presented so that I can show the students doing these things? Remember, it is students who must do these things and NOT THE TEACHER. Several failing students have presented lessons where the teacher helps the students to collect and aggregate the data; but do you see where it says in the rubric above that it can be the student **or** the teacher? Adjust accordingly!

The last part of this rubric seems like a "no brainer" but I've seen students fail this part. Ask yourself, is one person wearing goggles? Are you?

Rubric 5

The first bulleted item is "The candidate monitors student understanding by eliciting student responses that require mathematical reasoning or problem solving strategies" (Elementary Math Rubrics, 2013). What does that mean for you? It means that while you are *discoursing* with students it's important that you ask them questions (while monitoring for comprehension during instruction) that require them to reason or problem-solve. In essence, their answers to your questions should immediately employ a foundational understanding of the skills that you have just taught them; those kinds of questions will show or prove to you that they understand the purpose behind the mathematics, e.g., "why is the area of a triangle ½ base times the height?" or "When solving equations, why do you have to perform the same operation to both sides?" Those types of questions move beyond rote memorization of multiplication facts. Since those types of question/answer interactions need to be included in the video, you should make a notation on the lesson plan so that you don't forget. I've indicated "reasoning question" below and added * to remain consistent with the previous video inclusions.

The last bullet in the instruction rubrics is "Candidate responses **build on student input to guide improvement** of students' understanding of mathematical concepts and discourse." That is a tough one to plan for in the lesson. What does that mean? According to PACT, that type of questioning not only requires the candidate (you) to pose questions that encourage intellectual thinking, but you will use the responses from the students as an assessment tool to make instructional decisions. What decisions? Well perhaps you are teaching a lesson and the students don't seem to be "getting it," so by asking questions and eliciting student responses, I assess that they will need a bit of remediation; I stop moving forward and take a moment to provide the necessary information for them to "get it" and pick up where I left off. Another example, a bad example, might include stopping the originally planned lesson to remediate for the rest of the lesson, but that should have been mitigated by a pretest… For now let's make sure that you ask at least one question during each section of the lesson plan that is of the assessment type and that you get enough information from them to determine student understanding.

Anticipating answers from students challenges all teachers, but it does mean that if students provide wrong answers or no answers, DON'T MOVE ON without addressing it first!

Science – Rubric 4 says "Strategies for intellectual engagement seen in the clips offer **structured opportunities** for students to **actively** collect, analyze, and interpret scientific data. These strategies reflect **attention to student characteristics, learning needs, and/or language needs. No potential safety problems** are visible in the videotapes." (Science Rubric 4, 2016)

There have been multiple failing science Teaching Events due to the fact that candidates have neglected to incorporate the need to "actively collect, analyze and interpret the scientific data." You must show all three of those things during the video. I believe one of the key words here is "actively." What does "actively" look like? Students must be engaged and seen collecting, analyzing and interpreting their own data; NOT THE TEACHER. Think about how you will need to compress those elements into your lesson plans such that during the video we see the students questioning, writing and making connections about their experiment and their data in order to make connections to their current lives.

The second part of the rubric is the same as in the Mathematics rubric 4; see above for more information. The last part of the rubric seems like a "no brainer" but it is definitely something to pay attention to… After you record, watch your video carefully to ensure that all students are following safely procedures as outlined in your lessons.

Figure 2.4

Day 1	Day 2	Day 3
Standard 1.1	Standard 1.2	Standard 1.3
Objective 1.1	Objective 1.2	Objective 1.3
Engagement *Prior knowledge* *Experiential or interests* *Receptive/productive*	Engagement *Prior knowledge* *Experiential or interests* *Receptive/productive*	Engagement *Prior knowledge* *Experiential or interests* *Receptive/productive*
Instruction *Conceptual understanding* *Procedural understanding?* *Math reasoning/reasoning question* *Scaffolding for subgroups* *Receptive/productive – ID* *Struggling learners* *Special Ed* *Gate* *CELDT 4* *CELDT 5* *Receptive/productive - ID*	Instruction *Procedural understanding* *Math reasoning/reasoning question* *Scaffolding for subgroups* *Receptive/productive – ID* *Struggling learners* *Special Ed* *Gate* *CELDT 4* *CELDT 5* *Receptive/productive - ID*	Instruction *Procedural understanding* *Math reasoning/reasoning question* *Scaffolding for subgroups* *Receptive/productive – ID* *Struggling learners* *Special Ed* *Gate* *CELDT 4* *CELDT 5* *Receptive/productive - ID*
Application/Independent *Receptive/productive - ID*	Application/Independent *Receptive/productive- ID*	Application/Independent *Receptive/productive - ID*
Assessment *Did I assess what I just taught?* *Receptive/productive*	Assessment *Did I assess what I just taught?* *Receptive/productive*	Assessment *Did I assess what I just taught?* *Receptive/productive*
Materials	Materials	Materials

Are you saying "Crap! That's a lot to cover in 15 minutes?" The answer here is that within each of the daily lessons, you'll need to include in your video at least one of each of the elements that have an asterisk next to it (there are several places where it's repeated).

> Science 5: The candidate monitors student understanding by eliciting student responses that require thinking about science concepts and the quality of the data. Candidate responses build on student input to guide improvement of students' abilities to collect, analyze, and interpret scientific data. (Science Rubric, 2015)

Just like in the Mathematics example provided, you will need to have Q&A time with your students regarding science concepts and the quality of their data. Think about when that might happen; can it be during the collection, analysis, or the interpretation of the data? Looking at the second part of this rubric, "candidate responses build on student input to guide improvement of students' abilities to collect, analyze, and interpret scientific data", then you should have the answer to the last question. If not, then the answer is yes, yes and yes. Getting back to the lesson plans, you will need to provide a host of questions that will enable your students to respond to science concepts during collection, analysis, and interpretation. Plan ahead which questions you will ask that will provide you with the needed answers that the rubric has asked for.

Planning for academic language

The last thing you'll need to plan for are the academic language rubrics. Historically, these rubrics and concepts are pretty tough to master. Let's break it down again…

What are language demands? It's the language that students will need to negotiate and communicate the learning in your classroom within the confines of the content area. If I ask a student to answer "what is the value of a quarter?" I am not only asking the student to give me the *cent* equivalent, but I am also asking the student to know what "value" means. What does that consideration mean for the teacher? You will generally teach the vocabulary of the lesson and it's pretty easy to remember to do this, but the students will also need to know the "other words" that you'll be using when teaching a particular concept. These words are generally embedded within the content of the lesson and are easily overlooked by the instructor.

Figure 2.5

EM11: How does the candidate identify the language demands of learning tasks and assessments relative to the students' current levels of academic language proficiency?	EM 12: How do the candidate's planning, instruction, and assessment support academic language development?
<ul><li>Candidate describes academic language strengths and needs of students at different levels of academic language proficiency.</li><li>The language genre(s) discussed are clearly related to the academic purpose of the learning segment and language demands are identified. **One or more linguistic features and/or textual resources of the genre are explicitly identified**.</li><li>Candidate identifies **essential vocabulary** for students to actively engage in specific language tasks.</li></ul>	<ul><li>The candidate's use of scaffolding or other support provides access to core content while also providing **explicit models, opportunities for practice, and feedback for students to develop further language proficiency** for selected genres and key linguistic features.</li><li>Candidate articulates why the instructional strategies chosen are likely to support **specific** aspects of students' language development for **different levels** of language proficiency.</li></ul>

Before moving on to the Planning commentary prompts we have one more area of concern to add to our lesson plan template; Academic Language. Before I go further, at one time Academic Language was the lowest scoring section in the Teaching Event throughout the state of California. We're doing a better job now, but as educators, we still need some work. I'd like you to take special care when planning and instructing students in the area of academic language. The first bulleted point on the Academic Language rubric is:

> *"Candidate describes academic language strengths and needs of students at different levels of academic language proficiency."* (Elementary Math Rubrics, 2013).

Unlike the rest of the rubrics in the Teaching Event, the Academic Language rubrics cover the **entire** event, viz. planning, instruction, assessment and reflections; make sure you've got yourself covered. Read and internalize the sentence again. Where would you describe the academic language strengths and needs of your students at all of their different levels? Remember when I asked you to "cut and paste your subgroup list?" Well, that bulleted item refers to your answers within the commentaries. If you've already done this "cutting and pasting" then you're ready to move on. If not, get to it!

The second bulleted item is:

> "The language genre(s) discussed are clearly related to the academic purpose of the learning segment and language demands are identified. **One or more linguistic features and/or textual resources of the genre are explicitly identified**". (Elementary Math Rubrics, 2013).

What does this mean? Let's break it down for better understanding. A language genre for elementary math may include "interpreting or representing mathematical meanings represented symbolically, graphically or linguistically; recounting computational procedures or strategies used to solve mathematical problems; evaluating or constructing mathematical arguments; explaining mathematical concepts, defining technical terms; engaging in collaborative and oral mathematical reasoning" (Elementary Math Rubrics, 2013). Essentially, the teaching event needs to include a few instances where students are asked to explain by productive language (speaking or writing) the content by interpreting, representing, recounting, evaluating, etc. You get the drift; you need to plan and implement instances where students are speaking or writing about the content in appropriate ways (check your rubrics for specific examples). I mentioned earlier that you need to plan; so get out your template and add that notation to it. But in which section should I add it? Should it be in the engagement section? Should it be in the instruction section? How about both? What about assessment? Should the students "use" the academic language there too? Yes, yes, yes, put it there too!

Figure 2.6

Day 1	Day 2	Day 3
Standard 1.1	Standard 1.2	Standard 1.3
Objective 1.1	Objective 1.2	Objective 1.3
Engagement *Prior knowledge* *Experiential or interests* **Receptive/productive* *Academic language strategy*	Engagement *Prior knowledge* *Experiential or interests* **Receptive/productive* *Academic language strategy*	Engagement *Prior knowledge* *Experiential or interests* **Receptive/productive* *Academic language strategy*

Instruction
*Conceptual understanding
Procedural understanding?
*Math reasoning/problem solving?
*Scaffolding for subgroups
  Struggling learners
  Special Ed
  Gate
  CELDT 4
  CELDT 5
*Receptive/productive – ID
Academic language strategy
	Instruction
	*Conceptual understanding?
	Procedural understanding
	*Math reasoning/problem solving?
	*Scaffolding for subgroups
	  Struggling learners
	  Special Ed
	  Gate
	  CELDT 4
	  CELDT 5
	*Receptive/productive – ID
	Academic language strategy
		Instruction
		Procedural understanding
		*Math reasoning
		*Scaffolding for subgroups
		  Struggling learners
		  Special Ed
		  Gate
		  CELDT 4
		  CELDT 5
		*Receptive/productive - ID
		Academic language strategy

Application/Independent **Receptive/productive - ID*	Application/Independent **Receptive/productive - ID*	Application/Independent **Receptive/productive - ID*
Assessment *Did I assess what I just taught?* *Receptive/productive* *Academic language strategy*	Assessment *Did I assess what I just taught?* *Receptive/productive* *Academic language strategy*	Assessment *Did I assess what I just taught?* *Receptive/productive* *Academic language strategy*
Materials	Materials	Materials

Figure 2.7 (see Appendix 2 for blank template)

Day	Learning Task/Activity	Purpose
Day 1	Review of homework	Activate prior knowledge of learning before the addition of new learning. Also a check for understanding of previous concepts.
	Discussion and questions to introduce new concept	Questions intended to use experiential background examples to activate thinking of prior concepts and then add to what the students have already learned
	Questions regarding conceptual knowledge	After activating prior knowledge students will add to their existing knowledge the application of multiplication of decimals through understanding of conceptual knowledge. Cognitive modeling ensures that visual and auditory learners can access the content.
	Guided modeling of problems	
Day 2		

Planning for Assessments

While most of the three rubrics in the Assessment section concentrate on analyzing student work, there are a couple of outlying elements that you need to address while you are planning. The main element here is the rubric you will use to determine student learning. Many of the past unsuccessful candidates failed because the rubrics they used were either not aligned with the objectives from the lessons or the rubrics lacked the necessary details to do a detailed analysis.

Before you draft your assessments, let's take a look at the level 3 rubrics in the assessment task:

- The criteria/rubric and analysis **focus on patterns of student errors, skills, and understandings** to analyze student learning in relation to standards and learning objectives.
- Specific patterns are identified for **individuals or subgroup(s)** in addition to the whole class.
- Next steps focus on improving student performance through **targeted support** to individuals and groups to address specific **identified-needs**.

- Next steps are **based on whole class patterns** of performance and **some patterns for individuals and/or subgroups** and are described in sufficient detail to understand them.
- Specific and timely **feedback helps the student understand what s/he has done well,** and provides **guidance for improvement.**
- Students need to demonstrate their thinking and it is difficult with multiple choice questions or single word response answers (from Making Good Choices)

After reading them over, I'd like you to read them again with another perspective that asks "what do I need to think about now during the planning phase of my Teaching Event?" Let's look at the first bulleted item. It basically says that you'll need to focus on patterns of errors, skills and understandings. In other words, you'll need a rubric that provides enough detail that you'll be able to focus on patterns of errors, skills and understandings! Take elementary mathematics as an example. The planning rubrics call for you to teach conceptual, procedural and reasoning knowledge. If I am to determine whether my students have understood the conceptual knowledge I just taught, shouldn't that be articulated in my rubric? Let's put this thought into a four-point chart for organization.

Do you love charts? I love charts!

Figure 2.8

	1	2	3	4
Conceptual knowledge				

What does your lesson objective indicate that you'll be teaching? Do you have a conceptual, procedural and reasoning component? OK, chart time! Wait, what else are we planning for? Did you say "academic language?" Hopefully yes! You will need to also measure the academic language gains that the students have made, not just the academic ones.

Figure 2.9

	1	2	3	4
Conceptual knowledge				
Procedural knowledge				
Math Reasoning				
Academic language				

All right, so now you have a basic guideline for what you will measure in your rubric. Now it's time for you to fill in the rubric criteria with enough detail that you will be able to determine what the students understood or misunderstood with respect to your lesson. A word to the wise here: I really hate it when students write rubrics with words such as "understand", "introduce," or any other words that fail to provide what concrete evidence you will use to score them. I've seen rubrics that say "students will understand …" Really, what are you planning on doing? Should you ask them "raise your hand if you don't understand what's going on..." How many hands do you think you'll see? Ask yourself, what determines concrete understanding based on your objective for your lesson?

I won't get into "introduce" because it is just plain stupid. What does "introduce" mean there? Do you envision your lesson starting with, "Hello class, this is my friend, Algebraic-conceptual-understanding, I hope that you'll get along"?

Preparing for the "Daily Reflections"

This is not your gratuitous reflection and don't treat it like some of the other reflections you have written for other purposes. This is not an "Oh, the lesson went well, I had a few bumps in flow, and I ran out of time…" The reflections are specific to your whole class, subgroups, and some individuals in the class with respect to both the academics and the language development of the students. Here are the requirements:

> *Record a **daily reflection** after teaching each lesson by responding to the following prompts: (TPEs 12, 13)*
> *What is working? What is not? For whom? Why? (Consider teaching and student learning with respect to both content and academic language development.)*
> *How does this reflection inform what you plan to do in the next lesson?*
> ***Daily reflections will be submitted with Task 5. Reflecting on Teaching & Learning.***
> (Elementary Mathematics Teaching Event Handbook (2013)

Let's think about this one for a moment, if you will need to report to me what is working or not, for whom and why, then the daily assessment (either hardcopy or monitoring) will need to be sufficiently detailed enough for you to report this data. Students often ask me if they will need a rubric for each day and the simple answer is no - but what if you did? Would it make it easier for you to report the daily data? Would it make it easier for you to make decisions about the next lesson? DUH!

Planning Prompts

These prompts come directly from the handbook and we'll take them one at a time. The recommended page allowance is pretty much on target, and as an author, you should consider that when writing the commentaries. You will also notice that there is NOT a one-to-one correspondence between the rubrics and the prompts. The planning section has three rubrics and the planning commentary has seven prompts. You should also note that the prompts do not directly ask you to write to your subgroups, but the rubrics do!

The first prompt reads:

What is the central focus of the learning segment? Apart from being present in the school curriculum, student academic content standards, or ELD standards, why is the content of the learning segment important for your particular students to learn? (TPE 1) (Elementary Mathematics Teaching Event Handbook, 2013)

The intent there is to make a connection to what you are teaching to a "bigger picture." Does this content have a real-world connection? Will the students use this content to do other things in the content area? Why is this important for the students to learn? For example, if I were to teach students adding and subtracting decimals, then I would have to link that content to using money in everyday life.

The second prompt reads:

Briefly describe the theoretical framework and/or research that inform your instructional design for developing your students' knowledge and abilities in both mathematics and academic language during the learning segment. (Elementary Mathematics Teaching Event Handbook, 2013)

Remember when I said to copy and paste your subgroups into every section of the prompts? Well now is the time to address them… Let me provide you with an example, an extreme example granted, but one nonetheless. Let's say I have a class of 20 students and 10 of them are blind and the other 10 have significant hearing loss. Would you say that I should scaffold instruction and be very choosy in selecting strategies that will work for this classroom population? Of course! **The teaching event specifically measures how capable you are to design, implement, execute and assess instruction to a specific population in both academics and academic language.** The extreme example should demonstrate the devotion required of us to address a "specific population."

The prompt asks for the theoretical framework or research that drives the planning for your teaching event. Each of the strategies you are using hopefully comes from research. You should consider a framework for each of your subgroups. For example, your English language learners are still working to acquire language, fluency, etc. and the strategies you will be using have come from a framework. What about your struggling learners? Will you use specific strategies to scaffold instruction for them? You bet! During your time in your credential program you were exposed a number of different frameworks from your coursework. You studied educational psychology where you learned about development and motivation, you took content area methodology courses where you studied specific ways to teach your content area and the list goes on and on. Go back through you previous textbooks, reread your notes from your courses and spend some time writing to the second prompt. If you'd like a bit of help with this, then take a look at Appendix 8. I've outlined a few frameworks as well as some authors that might be helpful for guiding you in the right direction.

The third prompt reads:
> *How do key learning tasks in your plans build on each other to support students' development of conceptual understanding, computational/procedural fluency, mathematical reasoning skills, and related academic language? Describe specific strategies that you will use to build student learning across the learning segment. Reference the instructional materials you have included, as needed. (TPEs 1, 4, 9)* (Elementary Mathematics Teaching Event Handbook, 2013)

Back in the planning section of this workbook and in figure 2.7 specifically, you wrote down the specific tasks you used from your lesson plans. Consider using that form to write to this prompt. This prompt is asking you to validate how each of the tasks build upon each other to support the learning of your students. You will need to address each of the areas (conceptual and procedural understanding as well as math reasoning.) You will also need to write to each of your subgroups (see rubrics for planning.) And remember that through a lesson or a unit, the progression of tasks and assessments will play a central role in your learning segment.

Let me provide you with an example for clarification. In figure 2.7, I wrote, "After activating prior knowledge, students will add to their existing knowledge the application of multiplication of decimals through understanding of conceptual knowledge. Cognitive modeling ensures that visual and auditory learners can access the content." My commentary might begin with something like this; "according to Social Cognitive Theory (Schunk, 2004), the use of cognitive modeling and observational learning, increases attention and retention for the auditory and visual learner as well as provides the rehearsal component for learners who struggle…"

> Science – *"How do key learning tasks in your plans build on each other to support student learning on science concepts, inquiry skills, and the development of related academic language? How will students use the science concepts and inquiry skills to make sense of one or more real world phenomena?..."* (Science Teaching Event Handbook, 2015)

OK, new word here, "inquiry." According to Wikipedia, "An **inquiry** is any process that has the aim of augmenting knowledge… or solving a problem." Essentially, how does your "roll-out" of tasks build upon one another to support student science learning while augmenting their knowledge or solving a problem, while supporting students' growth of science concepts and the relationship they have with real world phenomena? Wow, that was a mouth full! It seems like that is an easy one to answer, but be careful about how you explain it.

The fourth prompt reads:
> *Given the description of students that you provided in Task 1.Context for Learning, how do your choices of instructional strategies, materials, technology, and the sequence of learning tasks reflect your students' backgrounds, interests, and needs? Be specific*

*about how your knowledge of **your** students informed the lesson plans, such as the choice of text or materials used in lessons, how groups were formed or structured, using student learning or experiences (in or out of school) as a resource, or structuring new or deeper learning to take advantage of specific student strengths. (TPEs 4,6,7,8,9)* (Elementary Mathematics Teaching Event Handbook, 2013)

Let's break that monster down so you don't missing anything. The first sentence, "given the description of students that you provided in Task 1, Context for Learning..." Could it mean that you will need to write to your subgroups that you previously identified? Yes, yes, yes. But wait, let's examine the rest of the sentence. It basically asks you to take one of your subgroups and describe how you chose the instructional strategies (see Appendix 4 for sample), materials and technology to teach the group of students. The sentence also reads, how you used the students' backgrounds, interests and needs to inform your teaching.

Let's go back to figure 2.5 for a minute. I asked you to inscribe backgrounds, interests and prior knowledge into your lesson plan template. If you have done that, then you should be prepared to write to this prompt. Let's take the subgroup of struggling learners; you will write to how you chose the strategies, materials and technology to help the students to structure new or deeper learning. Also, for this particular subgroup, you will explain how you implemented prior knowledge, backgrounds and interests to inform your teaching. After you have completed that subgroup, you will then need to write to the other subgroups that you have identified. Sounds like a lot of writing? Yes it is. Good thing we started early!

The fifth prompt reads:

> Math – *For this learning segment, identify students' possible or common errors. How will your assessments and lessons to identify and address possible misconceptions and errors?* (Elementary Mathematics Teaching Event Handbook, 2015)

By the time you are ready to record a lesson for your students, you should have some knowledge of how they perform Mathematics and what type of errors seem to go on and on. An example might be before you teach long division; you might have to review subtraction. Many times, students will forget that they have to "borrow" and just find the difference between the two numbers. Take for instance this equation, $521 - 329 = ?$ Students have often provided the answer as 208. Instead of borrowing from the two to make 11, they just find the difference between the two numbers and get eight.

If you can't answer this prompt off the top of your head, then go back and take a look at their old work and figure it out!

> Science – *For this learning segment, identify students' possible common sense understandings or misconceptions that contrast with accepted scientific understandings.*

How will you detect and attempt to change these common sense understandings or misconceptions? (Science Teaching Event Handbook, 2015)

Unlike the earlier example of mathematics and subtraction, Science has other stuff going on that will inhibit the learning of your students. Yes, you will likely have stuff to review before you give your lesson, but that's not all you should consider before beginning. There are common myths or misconceptions about Science, that your students may have heard and may believe they understand. For example, lightning never strikes the same place twice. Have you heard this? Do you think it's true? Then how do you explain that the Empire State Building gets struck about 25 times a year? Or if you drop something on the floor, you have five seconds to retrieve it before germs are able to adhere to it. That one is especially yucky! You get the message… Take a moment while you are planning to think of things that your students might consider are true that are really myths or misconceptions.

The sixth prompt reads:

Consider the language demands[3] of the oral and written tasks in which you plan to have students engage as well as the various levels of English language proficiency related to classroom tasks as described in the Context Commentary. (TPE 7)

a. *Identify words and phrases (if appropriate) that you will emphasize in this learning segment. Why are these important for students to understand and use in completing classroom tasks in the learning segment? Which students?*

b. *What oral and/or written academic language (organizational, stylistic, and/or grammatical features) will you teach and/or reinforce?*

c. *Explain how specific features of the learning and assessment tasks in your plan, including your own use of language, support students in learning to understand and use these words, phrases (if appropriate), and academic language. How does this build on what your students are currently able to do and increase their abilities to follow and/or use different types of text and oral formats?* (Elementary Mathematics Teaching Event Handbook, 2013)

Although lengthy, that prompt is pretty straightforward. From your list of linguistic subgroups, you will need to answer all of the questions with respect to them. Remember that the teaching event is designed to see how well you can scaffold instruction to meet the demands of your particular classroom population.

The seventh prompt reads:

Explain how the collection of assessments from your plan allows you to evaluate your students' learning of specific student standards/objectives and provide feedback to

---

[3] Language demands can be related to vocabulary, features of text types such as problem solutions or mathematical notation, or other language demands such as language conventions and structures within mathematical reasoning. For early readers/writers, this will include sound-symbol correspondence and a word or number as a text but might also involve the development of oral skills which are antecedents to reading and writing, oral narratives, and explanations.

students on their learning. (TPEs 2, 3) (Elementary Mathematics Teaching Event Handbook, 2013)

Assessments come in many different forms; should you write about your subgroups and how you measured their learning? What do you think? You will likely monitor understanding during the lesson with a thumbs up or down, use white boards, ask comprehension questions during the lesson (most likely several times), have some sort of "worksheet" or "exit ticket" for the students to complete, a formative or summative test and the list goes on... The goal here is to be able to directly measure the learning objectives or standards during and after executing each of the lesson plans. You will need to go back to your lesson plans and "see" where you have written to the assessments. If you lesson plan isn't detailed enough for you to "see" this then you might consider revising them so that your assessor knows for certain that you have provided assessments throughout your learning segment.

After identifying all of the assessments in each one of your lesson plans, then match them to the daily objective of the lesson. Are you measuring the objective directly, do you have other stuff you are measuring and have you measured the entire objective? That is often where students fall down on their writing; they don't relate the assessments directly back to the objective of the lesson. If you are in doubt, then a helpful hint might be to copy and paste your lesson objectives into this prompt and then begin your writing around the objectives, handling each one separately.

The eighth prompt reads:

> *Describe any teaching strategies you have planned for your students who have identified educational needs (e.g., English learners, GATE students, students with IEPs). Explain how these features of your learning and assessment tasks will provide students access to the curriculum and allow them to demonstrate their learning. (TPEs 9. 12)* (Elementary Mathematics Teaching Event Handbook, 2013)

This prompt may seem a bit repetitive but it focuses on how the learning and assessment tasks work together to provide your students with access. Will you need to include commentary about your subgroups? Yes! It has been my experience that candidates have difficulty expressing how their assessments provided students with the ability to demonstrate their learning. Let's go back to the "extreme" example. If I have 10 blind students, then giving them a paper and pencil test is out of the question. So ask yourself, will my English Learners be able to read and comprehend the questions on the test? Will my struggling learners be able to do the same? What I'm saying here is how will you know whether you have measured the students' content knowledge or their ability to read and comprehend English? So give it some thought before you put into your lesson plan that the students will have to complete an "exit ticket" before leaving class; will all of your students be able to read and comprehend the directions? How about the very words in the questions?

Words of "Planning" Wisdom from passing candidates:

- Always start with the lesson plans. Once you have lesson plans done you can go in and add to them to include things you might have forgotten while preparing them. It took about one week for me to perfect my lesson plans then another week to write the commentary for the PACT.
- Don't plan after you teach! Plan with lots of details!
- Make sure you do the assignments when the professor tells you. Also make sure you have enough time to proofread it and make corrections.
- Start on this portion as soon as possible, granted you will change it a million times and it will look nothing like it did at first, the more you work with it the better. Choose your topic early on and use that to guide as many assignments in other classes as possible so that you can get feedback, sources, and ideas.
- I found this the most difficult section. I had to make lots of changes as I looked at the rubrics and the prompts. GET STARTED EARLY!
- I believe that I was successful in passing the PACT because I started to prepare for it early. I used the rubrics to guide my writing because, obviously, that's how you'll be assessed! I also used the PACT handbook which was very helpful. Take lots of time writing each section and be thorough. Edit over and over again. DO NOT START LATE as many of my classmates did. Be organized, know what you need to complete, set a schedule of goals, and ask for help. Most questions that my classmates had about the PACT were answered in the rubric and handbook. Keep those documents on hand, and become friends with them to be successful.
- Take time to research your citations and make a reference list while you find your citations. Get your sub-groups and plan around those sub-groups. Work on your PACT throughout the semester because it takes about a good 25-30 hours to complete.
- The planning section should show why you planned your lesson and who influenced you. Think about the students in your class and why your lesson is helping them.

CHAPTER 3
INSTRUCTING STUDENTS & SUPPORTING LEARNING

Readings
- Teaching Event Handbook – pgs. 11-13
- Making Good Choices pgs. 8 – 12

Suggested Instructional Activities
- Watch YouTube videos or any other teaching videos on the internet and have the candidates score them according to the instruction rubrics (instructor should view them ahead of time and select a couple of fictitious subgroups). Encourage a discussion of appropriate strategies for subgroups and rubric scores.
- Peer-review Instruction Commentaries (see Appendix 7)
- In small groups, encourage candidates to share their videos scoring them according to the instruction rubrics and matching the video to the lesson plan

The Teaching Event Handbook describes this section as:

"The Instructing Students & Supporting Learning task illustrates how you work with your students to improve their understanding of mathematical concepts and their ability to engage in mathematical discourse. It provides evidence of your ability to engage students in meaningful mathematics tasks and monitor their understanding."

Candidates have told me that videotaping themselves is both "weird" and "nerve-racking." I recommend that you record yourself several times so that you have several lessons from which to choose. I strongly suggest that you record a couple of times before you actually teach your learning segment. This is not only an opportunity for you to practice and to become less stressed but to also give the students an opportunity to get used to the camera. I have seen many videos where students are making faces or waving to the camera, sleeping on their desk, throwing an occasional gang sign, putting on makeup or refusing to speak. Not only do you want to avoid those things, but you will also need to consider if you can edit your video so that you will be able to include all of the components that are necessary for you to score well on the Teaching Event. The prerecorded lessons will also provide valuable information to you about camera angles and best places to set-up a camera so students can be heard; basically, work out the logistics.

One of my students told me that the first time she recorded she went home to see if she was able to include all of the components of the rubric. She found that she was short by two minutes on her second clip. That feedback enabled her to restructure her lesson plan a bit and incorporate all of the necessary elements of the rubric.

You will need to get permission slips from each of the student's parents in order to record them. I have found that most districts have a specific video permission slip, so my best recommendation is to ask the school secretary or administrator. Also consider getting the permission slips out early. Having to rearrange seating just before recording can easily upset the students and then you will have worry about classroom management while you are taping.

Below you will find the table indicating how long you will be able to record and requirements for submission. While the teaching event says you can video whole class or small group, the rule from the PACT folks is that there needs to be a minimum of 12 students.

Figure 3.1

Content	Video Clip (Times) *TASK 3*
Bilingual Elementary Math	One or two video clips of no more than fifteen minutes total.
Elementary Math	One or two video clips of no more than fifteen minutes total.
Secondary Art	Three video clips (1) = 5 Min., (2) = 10 Min., and (3) = 10 Min.
Secondary English Language Arts	Two video clips of no more than ten minutes each.
Secondary History Social Science	Two video clips of no more than ten minutes each.
Secondary Mathematics	One or two video clips of no more than twenty minutes total.
Secondary Music	One or two video clips of no more than twenty minutes total.
Secondary Physical Education	One or two video clips of no more than fifteen minutes total.
Secondary Science	Two video clips of no more than twenty minutes total.
Secondary World Language	Two video clips of no more than ten minutes, each.

Instruction Rubrics Figure 3.2 (Elementary Math Rubrics, 2013)

EM4: Engaging Students in Learning. How does the candidate actively engage students in their own understanding of mathematical concepts and discourse?	EM 5: Monitoring Student Learning During Instruction. How does the candidate monitor student learning during instruction and respond to student questions, comments, and needs?
• Strategies for intellectual engagement seen in the clip(s) offer **structured opportunities** for students to **actively develop** their own understanding of mathematical concepts and discourse. • These strategies reflect **attention to student characteristics, learning needs, and/or language needs**.	• The candidate monitors student understanding by eliciting student responses that require mathematical reasoning or problem solving strategies. • Candidate responses **build on student input to guide improvement** of students' understanding of mathematical concepts and discourse.

We have dealt with EM4 and the first bulleted item in EM5 in the Planning section of this guide. Hopefully you have planned for the "structured opportunities," "attention to student characteristics" and "eliciting student responses…" So let's deal with what is left. The second item in EM 5 reads "Candidate responses build on student input to guide improvement of students' understanding of mathematical concepts and discourse." (Elementary Mathematics Rubrics, 2013). What does that mean? It means that through questioning and comments from the students, the candidate responds to students' answers and comments to help improve their understanding of the content being taught. As teachers we constantly check for understanding through different means before moving on to the next topic. It might come from questions, having student reiterate information, use of white boards, etc., but the bottom line is that we are there to teach students. All students. Sometimes candidates are so nervous about recording their lesson that a student will give incorrect answers and the candidate moves forward without addressing the misconception. That can be one of the gravest offenses. Essentially, you will build upon what the students are saying to get them to understand and deepen their understanding of the content. Perhaps you might think of it as "thinking out loud." For example, you ask the students in your class what is $1 + 2 = ?$ The majority of the students yell out 3, but you have one or two students who say 2. So you pause for a moment, change gears a bit, and respond to the thinking behind the problem. You may give a few more examples to check to ensure the previously inaccurate students are now "getting it."

Instruction Prompts

First prompt reads:

> *Other than what is stated in the lesson plan(s), what occurred immediately prior to and after the video clip(s) that is important to know in order to understand and interpret the interactions between and among you and your students? Please provide any other information needed to interpret the events and interactions in the video clip(s). (Teaching Event Handbook – Elementary Mathematics, 2013).*

This information just provides the assessor with a frame of reference about where the video occurred in your lesson plan. It is pretty straightforward but remember that what you write here is not evidence to be scored on the instruction rubrics. Don't say stuff like "I taught the conceptual learning portion of the lesson plan and then in the video you will see…" Remember that you will be scored solely on what is seen in the video.

Second prompt reads:

> *Describe any routines or working structures of the class (e.g., group work roles, class discussion norms) that were operating in the learning task(s) seen on the video clip(s). If specific routines or working structures are new to the students, how did you prepare students for them? (TPE 10)* (Teaching Event Handbook – Elementary Mathematics, 2013).

Again, pretty straightforward, but include details like strategic grouping for cooperative groups, seminar style discussions, etc.

Third prompt reads:

> *In the instruction seen in the clip(s), how did you further the students' knowledge and skills and engage them intellectually in understanding mathematical concepts and*

participating in mathematical discourse? Provide examples of both general strategies to address the needs of all of your students and strategies to address specific individual needs. (TPEs 1, 2, 4, 5, 7, 11) (Elementary Mathematics Teaching Event Handbook, 2013).

Science – *In the instruction seen in the clips, how did you further the students' knowledge and skills and engage them intellectually while collecting, analyzing, and interpreting data from a scientific inquiry? Provide examples of both general strategies to address the needs of all of your students and strategies to address specific individual needs. (TPEs 1, 2, 4, 5, 7, 11)* (Science Teaching Event Handbook, 2015)

If you spent the correct amount of time planning and following your lesson plan for the video portion of the Teaching Event, then you should be able to go directly back to your lessons and provide the examples of strategies. One of the exercises I give to my candidates is to mark on a hardcopy of the lesson plan (in the margin) and note all of the strategies to the side. Then I ask the students to watch their video and write down all of the strategies that they see. The candidates should then go back and include anything they included when teaching the lesson to the lesson plan. Often as teachers, when we read the faces of the students and see puzzlement, we stop and check for understanding. What happens next is directly dependent upon how well the students do after the check for understanding.

Fourth prompt reads:

> *Given the language abilities of your students as described in Task 1. Context for Learning, provide examples of language supports seen in the clips that help your students understand the content and/or academic language central to the lesson. (TPEs 4, 7)* (Teaching Event Handbook – Elementary Mathematics, 2013).

That prompt is just asking you to pull the examples out that you provided for language supports for the students. Do you think you should write to your subgroups? Hmmm…

Fifth prompt reads:

> *Describe the strategies you used to monitor student learning during the learning task shown on the video clip(s). Cite one or two examples of what students said and/or did in the video clip(s) or in assessments related to the lesson that indicated their progress toward accomplishing the lesson's learning objectives. (TPEs 2, 3)* (Teaching Event Handbook – Elementary Mathematics, 2013).

Here it is important that you are able to hear the students in the video. I find that candidates often discuss the assessments in the video, but they don't relate them back to the lesson's objective. Now that you know, reread the lesson objective and go and find the right comments!

Writing the "Daily Reflections"

As stated previously, this is not your gratuitous reflection and don't treat it like some of the other reflections you have written for other purposes. This is not an "Oh, the lesson went well, I had a few bumps in flow, and I ran out of time…" The reflections are specific to your whole class, subgroups, and some individuals in the class with respect to both the academics and the language development of the students. Here are the requirements again:

> Record a **daily reflection** after teaching each lesson by responding to the following prompts: (TPEs 12, 13)
> What is working? What is not? For whom? Why? (Consider teaching and student learning with respect to both content and academic language development.)
> How does this reflection inform what you plan to do in the next lesson?
> **Daily reflections will be submitted with Task 5. Reflecting on Teaching & Learning.**
> (Elementary Mathematics Teaching Event Handbook (2013)):

If you will need to report to your instructor what is working (or not) for whom and why, then the daily assessment (either hardcopy or monitoring) will need to be sufficiently detailed enough for you to report that data. Students often ask me if they will need a rubric for each day and the simple answer is no - but what if you did? Would it make it easier for you to report the daily data? Would it make it easier for you to make decisions about the next lesson? Would it be easier for you to answer the question? DUH!

OK, now that I have repeated myself, I'm hoping that you understand how important this part of the reflection is… My recommendation to you is to write your reflections right away. If you have to, take the camera that you just recorded your lesson on and speak into the camera to capture your immediate feelings about the lesson. Go home, crunch the data and write your reflection.

What does the last sentence "how does this reflection inform what you plan to do in the next lesson?" mean to you? Should you teach a lesson, reflect immediately after the lesson, crunch the data, and write the reflection within hours of teaching? Yes! The last sentence is asking you to make informed decisions about what just happened in the lesson. If you need to make changes, and most of you will, then you will need to go back and modify tomorrow's lesson. Let's say you don't adjust your lesson for the next day, what message does that send to the assessor? That you love your students so much that you don't want to make them revisit the same material or that you don't give a crap and just want to move on… Of course there are instances where you will not need to adjust the lesson for the next day, but for the majority of us, we make changes daily.

Words of "Instruction" Wisdom from passing candidates:

- Stay calm, natural, and ask a ton of questions! People made me soooo nervous with the video, which reflected on my video performance, but if you are prepared and just do what you do normally, you will be fine! Asking a lot of questions and videotaping a few lessons, not just one, will give you the opportunity to have choices and pick the best one. You would be surprised; the video I thought went the worst ended up being the best! It was filled with questions, informal assessments, and hands on materials.

- Video EVERYDAY. Show your video to friends/classmates because they will see things you don't. Don't over stress on what clips, pick the right ones, but move on.

- Video every one of your lessons and every period you plan to teach the lessons. This gives you plenty of options to make sure you have exactly what you need.

- Write after every lesson! Type it up and edit it; it saves so much time and keeps your brain focused and on track.

- Make sure you do a good job of clearly presenting your lesson in a manner that clearly shows your rationale during the planning phase, during the teaching event (with adjustments based on how the previous day went. this is important!), and then what you would change as a result if you had the chance to teach this lesson again.

- This was the easiest sections for me to write. As I watched my video, I took note of EVERY strategy I used and the time in video. It made the writing for this section easy and efficient.

- Make sure to address all the needs of all your subgroups, it's important to understand that your class is composed of diverse learners and when you are completing this section, make sure to utilize different strategies that address these specific needs.

CHAPTER 4
ASSESSING STUDENT LEARNING

Readings

- Teaching Event Handbook pages 14 – 17
- Making Good Choices pages 13 – 17

Suggested Instructional Activities

- Peer-review the candidate authored rubrics
- Peer-review commentaries (see Appendix 7)
- In class – I generally have candidates bring in their student samples. These are shared with other candidates and with post-it notes I have the students make comments on them as to why the student missed the problem/answer. For Elementary and Secondary Mathematics, I have the students analyze the student work by determining whether it was a conceptual, procedural, or reasoning error. This can be done for all content areas. We spend about 20 minutes on this exercise and when completed the papers are returned to the original candidate and then it is up to them how they will aggregate and disaggregate the data from the student work and the comments made by other teacher candidates.

The Teaching Event Handbook describes this section as:

"The Assessment of Student Learning task illustrates how you diagnose student learning needs through your analysis of student work samples. It provides evidence of your ability to 1) select an assessment tool and criteria that are aligned with your central focus, student standards, and learning objectives; 2) analyze student performance on an assessment in relation to student needs and the identified learning objectives; 3) provide feedback to students; and 4) use the analysis to identify next steps in instruction for the whole class and individual students." (Teaching Event Handbook – Elementary Mathematics, 2013)

Let's look at the rubrics for the assessment section. (Elementary Mathematics Rubrics, 2013)

EM 6: Analyzing Student Work From an Assessment. How does the candidate demonstrate an understanding of student performance with respect to standards/objectives?	EM 7: Using Assessment to Inform Teaching. How does the candidate use the analysis of student learning to prose next steps in instruction?	EM 8: Using Feedback to Promote Student Learning. What is the quality of feedback to students?
• The criteria/rubric and analysis **focus on patterns of student errors, skills, and understandings** to analyze	• Next steps focus on improving student performance through **targeted support** to individuals and	Specific and timely **feedback helps the student understand what s/he has done well**, and provides **guidance for improvement.**

student learning in relation to standards and learning objectives. • Specific patterns are identified for **individuals or subgroup(s)** in addition to the whole class.	groups to address specific **identified-needs**. • Next steps are **based on whole class patterns** of performance and **some patterns for individuals and/or subgroups** and are described in sufficient detail to understand them	

What I hear from passing candidates is that the more detailed the rubric you use for assessment, the easier it will be to write to the commentaries. I couldn't agree more. I think you'll see by the end of this chapter what I mean.

Let's take a look at the two bulleted points in rubrics EM6 and EM7.
You are looking for a number of things here. What do you know so far? Let's list them out so that you can see the bigger picture:

1. You based your lessons on conceptual knowledge, procedural knowledge and mathematical reasoning (from the handbook and PACT rubric) for mathematics so you'll need to include measurements of these. For other content areas, check the planning rubrics in your specific subject
2. Need to focus on the academic language of the lesson (from the handbook and the PACT rubrics)
3. You will need to include beginning to proficient levels of academic achievement
4. Need to base your criteria on the lesson's objectives (from the PACT rubric)
5. Need to provide evaluative criteria or rubric (from the handbook)
6. Need to focus on patterns of student errors, skills and understandings (from the PACT rubric)
7. You will need to discuss partial understandings
8. Students need to demonstrate their thinking, and it is difficult with multiple choice questions or single word response answers (from Making Good Choices)
9. You will need to be specific enough in your evaluative criteria such that you can discuss and be specific about next steps (from all three sources)

Ok, lots of stuff there, but what can you determine from that list? It seems to me that you need a very specific rubric (so you can disaggregate the data for errors, partial understandings and skills) that has multiple levels of proficiency, is based on the content elements from the lesson plans (you wrote to them in the planning) and will need to include items that were included so that students can demonstrate understanding (see Appendix 6 for suggestions). Now that you have a rough idea of what should be included, let's deal with that list.

You based your lessons on conceptual, procedural, and mathematical reasoning, so let's take this opportunity to insert item #1 into a rubric template. (For other content areas, see the planning rubrics for specific content.) Item #2 says that there should be a focus on academic language, so insert this now (see figure 2.9 below). Remember, we are just filling in a draft template and you can change the headings in the first column later. Items #3 is taken care of in the template below (ratings 1 to 4).

Item #4 says that you will need to base your criteria on the lesson's objectives and #5 says you will provide the evaluative criteria for the rubric. Take a look back at the lesson's objectives. As an example, let's say your lesson's objective is "students will be able to sort and classify shapes/objects (2D and 3D) by attribute." So conceptually we want the students to be able to understand what attributes are and what role they play in describing the shapes/objects. I might want to determine what the highest level of achievement will be and work my way down the rubric. In finding attributes I will want students to analyze the shapes/objects, determine what attributes the shapes have and be able to describe the shape using appropriate terminology. In figure 2.9, you will find an example of what might be expected by candidates based on their learning segment and lesson plans.

Figure 2.9 (from planning section)

Assessment Rubric	1	2	3	4
Conceptual Understanding	Students have difficulty providing a definition for attributes despite prompting. Students will be able to correctly identify 6 shapes and provide some detail descriptors for the shape	Students will be able to correctly provide a definition for attribute in their own words. Students will be able to correctly identify 6 shapes/objects and analyze each of the shapes with 4 out of the 6 designated descriptors	Students will be able to correctly provide a definition for attribute in their own words and provide an example(s) to demonstrate this understanding. Students will be able to correctly identify 6 shapes/objects and analyze each of the shapes with 5 out of the 6 designated descriptors	Students will be able to correctly provide a detailed definition for attribute in their own words and provide an example(s) to demonstrate this understanding. Students will be able to correctly identify 6 shapes/objects and analyze each of the shapes according to the number of **faces**, **edges**, **vertices**, and **bases** as well as **color** and **size**.
Procedural Understanding	Students will be able to correctly sort shapes/objects	Students will be able to correctly sort shapes/objects	Students will be able to correctly sort shapes/objects by 5 out of the 6	Students will be able to correctly sort shapes/objects by the number of faces, edges,

	in 3 or less cases	by 4 out of the 6 designated descriptors	designated descriptors	vertices, bases, color and size
Math Reasoning	Students will be able to apply their conceptual understanding of attributes to solve problems using special quadrilaterals and other not previously taught shapes but lacks an explanation of how previous problems were related	Students will be able to apply their conceptual understanding of attributes to solve problems using special quadrilaterals and other not previously taught shapes as well as provide an brief explanation of how previous problems were related describing how some of the elements that are the same and different	Students will be able to apply their conceptual understanding of attributes to solve problems using special quadrilaterals and other not previously taught shapes as well as provide an explanation of how previous problems were related describing elements that are the same and different	Students will be able to apply their conceptual understanding of attributes to solve problems using special quadrilaterals and other not previously taught shapes as well as provide a detail rich explanation of how previous problems were related describing elements that are the same and different
Academic Language (faces, edges, vertices, bases, size, color…)	Students use some appropriate terminology and have substituted other words to describe…	Students will use appropriate terminology to describe some of the shapes/objects and be able to ….	Students will use appropriate terminology to describe most of the shapes/objects and be able to ….	Students will use appropriate terminology to describe each of the shapes/objects and be able to ….

If you provide a detailed rubric and include all of the items from the lesson plan's objective then for items #6 and #7, the focus on patterns of student errors, skills and understandings as well as partial understandings should be apparent from the students' scores in each of the areas; if it isn't then consider revising your rubric to include more details…

Item #8 will be difficult for you to describe if you didn't ask the students appropriate questions; again, plan ahead. Item #9 will be based on your findings from the assessment that you gave to the students and should align with your rubric. Let's imagine for a moment that you have completed the previous rubric with all levels of achievement explicitly described. If I were to take this rubric and then add information (in example 2.9a) on how each of my subgroups scored, then it will give me a good look at how my students performed on the assessment.

Figure 2.9a

Assessment Rubric	1	2	3	4
Conceptual Understanding	Whole class – 10% CELDT 4 – 10% CELDT 5 – 25% Special Ed – 50% GATE – 0% Struggling – 50%	Whole class – 30% CELDT 4 – 50% CELDT 5 – 35% Special Ed – 20% GATE – 0% Struggling – 25%	Whole class – 40% CELDT 4 – 30% CELDT 5 – 15% Special Ed – 20% GATE – 40% Struggling – 20%	Whole class 20% CELDT 4 – 10% CELDT 5 – 5% Special Ed – 10% GATE – 60% Struggling – 5%
Procedural Understanding	CELDT 4 – 0% CELDT 5 – 0% Special Ed – 0% GATE – 0% Struggling – 0%	CELDT 4 – 10% CELDT 5 – 5% Special Ed – 10% GATE – 0% Struggling – 55%	CELDT 4 – 80% CELDT 5 – 75% Special Ed – 85% GATE – 60% Struggling – 40%	CELDT 4 – 10% CELDT 5 – 20% Special Ed – 5% GATE – 40% Struggling – 5%
Math Reasoning	Whole class – 20% CELDT 4 – 50% CELDT 5 – 60% Special Ed – 50% GATE – 0% Struggling – 50%	Whole class – 40% CELDT 4 – 30% CELDT 5 – 20% Special Ed – 30% GATE – 0% Struggling – 50%	Whole class – 30% CELDT 4 – 10% CELDT 5 – 10% Special Ed – 10% GATE – 40% Struggling – 50%	Whole class – 20% CELDT 4 – 10% CELDT 5 – 10% Special Ed – 0% GATE – 60% Struggling – 50%
Academic Language (faces, edges …)	Whole class – 10% CELDT 4 – 20% CELDT 5 – 20% Special Ed – 30% GATE – 0% Struggling – 30%	Whole class – 20% CELDT 4 – 40% CELDT 5 – 20% Special Ed – 20% GATE – 10% Struggling – 40%	Whole class – 20% CELDT 4 – 20% CELDT 5 – 25% Special Ed – 50% GATE – 10% Struggling – 10%	Whole class – 50% CELDT 4 – 20% CELDT 5 – 35% Special Ed – 0% GATE – 80% Struggling – 20%

What does the rubric/assessment data tell you? Let's take it one row at a time. How did my students do as learners in terms of understanding the conceptual knowledge I taught them? Who "got" it and who didn't? If your descriptions were detailed enough then you would be able to discuss your students' understandings, misunderstandings, and partial understandings. You don't have to be an expert to know that more students had trouble with conceptual understanding than procedural. What else do you see? Consider making a list of what the data tells you and discuss each item within the assessment commentaries.

The next steps (item #9) should also be apparent. If the students did poorly in conceptual understanding, then you'll teach the parts of conceptual understanding that they missed. If they did poorly in reasoning, then re-teach that! Get it? Often candidates will not analyze the student work properly and when the students make numerous errors (let's say conceptual errors) the candidate will erroneously teach the procedure the next day, when in fact the students did just fine procedurally.

EM 8 rubric is about feedback. It states:

> Specific and timely **feedback helps the student understand what s/he has done well**, and provides **guidance for improvement.** (Elementary Math Rubrics, 2013)

Key words here are specific and timely. As for specific, you should be able to provide constructive feedback to the student, but it will need to be in a well-documented place. It can be in the video, on student papers or verbally to the student. It should be constructive feedback designed so that the student can receive it, interpret what you meant and then go forth and get the correct answer or at the very least, move forward. If it is verbally you will need to transcribe your conversation with the student so that you can provide specific examples.

As for timely; what does this mean? According to Webster's Dictionary timely means "happening at the correct or most useful time: not happening too late." Pedagogically speaking I think Webster is right. The most useful time is when the students are continuing to work on the same content. It doesn't mean that you sit on their uncorrected work for a week or two and then give it back to them and have them make sense of it.

Let's take a look at the prompts. The first prompt reads:

> *Identify the specific standards/objectives measured by the assessment chosen for analysis. You may just cite the appropriate lesson(s) if you are assessing all of the standards/objectives listed.* (Teaching Event Handbook – Elementary Mathematics, 2013)

You will need to identify the specific standards or objective that your analysis was based. You may refer back to a lesson by stating "the analysis was done in lesson one" or you can list the standards or objectives again. From an assessor's view, I like having the objectives listed again here. Think about it: Do you want your assessor to be happy when scoring your teaching event? Obviously do what you think will be easiest for the assessor. While all assessors are trained and calibrated, it is easier if you just list it, plus it saves me from having to go back to your original lesson plans to find it.

I often have candidates ask which should they list, the standards or the objectives? Let's think about this for a moment. Which is more directly related to your lesson, the standards or the objectives? If you list a standard and have not taught the whole standard for the lesson, then it can be misleading to the assessor.

The second prompt reads:

> *Create a summary of student learning across the whole class relative to your evaluative criteria (or rubric). Summarize the results in narrative and/or graphic form (e.g., table or chart). Attach your rubric or evaluative criteria, and note any changes from what was planned as described in Planning commentary, prompt 6. (You may use the optional chart provided following the Assessment Commentary prompts to provide the evaluative criteria, including descriptions of student performance at different levels.) (TPEs 3, 5)* (Teaching Event Handbook – Elementary Mathematics, 2013)

If you have a detailed rubric then answering this prompt shouldn't be too difficult. You will have all of your data aggregated for the whole class and disaggregated for each of your subgroups. Will you need to write to your subgroups? Let me ask you what you think "... including descriptions of student performance at different levels" mean? The only additional item that you will need to discuss here is to note any changes you made to your original assessment or evaluative criteria.

The third prompt reads:

> *Discuss what most students appear to understand well, and, if relevant, any misunderstandings, confusions, or needs (including a need for greater challenge) that were apparent for some or most students. Cite evidence to support your analysis from the three student work samples you selected. (TPE 3)* (Teaching Event Handbook – Elementary Mathematics, 2013)

Again, the first part of this prompt should be relatively easy to answer if you have a detailed rubric and have disaggregated your data properly. You should also be aware of "…for some or most students" means… Do you think it means you should discuss your subgroups? The second half calls for you to provide three student work samples. So let's think about this for a moment. You will need to provide only three student work samples that are reflective of the problems the students had with the content. Let me give you an example for clarification. If I use the previous mathematics example the students may have had difficulty with:

1. Providing a definition for attributes for the three dimensional objects
2. Understanding that shapes/objects can be sorted by each of the attributes (3D)
3. Understanding how a rectangle and a rectangular prism are alike
4. Correctly counting the number of faces on cones, cylinders, and rectangular prisms
5. Using appropriate terminology for vertices (corner)

Now that you have a list of the difficulties students' had, you will need to choose three samples. The samples you choose have to be reflective of all of the items we listed above; ALL of them. Those samples are provided as evidence that you have a clear understanding of how your students are doing with respect to the curriculum you just taught. So choose your samples wisely. And don't forget, one of your samples needs to be from your EL student.

Another question I get from candidates is "should the samples come from each or some of my identified subgroups?" Let's think for a minute… Will you discuss how your subgroups did in prompt 2 and 3? Well, what do you think? In some cases students in your subgroups will overlap. Let's say that some of your EL CELDT 5 students (language subgroup) will also be in your GATE (academic subgroup). This will give you the ability to use one student sample to discuss three of the five difficulties that the class had.

The fourth prompt reads:

> *From the three students whose work samples were selected, choose two students, at least one of which is an English Learner. For these two students, describe their prior knowledge of the content and their individual learning strengths and challenges (e.g., academic development, language proficiency, special needs). What did you conclude about their learning during the learning segment? Cite specific evidence from the work samples and from other classroom assessments relevant to the same evaluative criteria (or rubric). (TPE 3)* (Teaching Event Handbook – Elementary Mathematics, 2013)

Remember when I said that a pretest might be a good idea? Well if you planned and implemented one you will have the information you will need to write to this prompt. Again, you will need to be really choosey about which student samples you decide to use. Here's the really tricky part. This prompt essentially requires that you have pretested and post-tested your students, and they both need to have the same evaluative criteria or rubric. Hmmm… good luck.

The fifth prompt reads:

> *What oral and/or written feedback was provided to individual students and/or the group as a whole (refer the reviewer to any feedback written directly on submitted student work samples)? How and why do your approaches to feedback support students' further learning? In what ways does your feedback address individual students' needs and learning goals? Cite specific examples of oral or written feedback, and reference the three student work samples to support your explanation.* (Teaching Event Handbook – Elementary Mathematics, 2013)

Remember when I said earlier that you need to provide constructive feedback to students? Well this prompt is asking for specific examples on what you wrote or said that is constructive and will support students to further their learning. Here again, you will need to choose your three student samples carefully.

The sixth prompt reads:

Based on the student performance on this assessment, describe the next steps for instruction for your students. If different, describe any individualized next steps for the two students whose individual learning you analyzed. These next steps may include a specific instructional activity or other forms of re-teaching to support or extend continued learning of objectives, standards, central focus, and/or relevant academic language for the learning segment. In your description, be sure to explain how these next steps follow from your analysis of the student performances. (TPEs 2, 3, 4, 13) (Teaching Event Handbook – Elementary Mathematics, 2013)

Again, if you have a detailed rubric and have disaggregated your data properly, that prompt shouldn't present too big of a challenge. Recall that this is not a gratuitous reflection: That prompt should reflect your data findings. In fact, please consider starting your paragraphs with "based on the data…"

When you add that additional requirement you should have the following for your three student samples:

1. Need to be indicative of your subgroups and their outcome performances
2. Reflect the difficulties your students had (trends)
3. Reflect what the students did well on or understood
4. Reflect the partial understandings your students exhibited
5. Need to be from at least one EL student
6. You will need to be able to provide constructive feedback either on the paper or verbally and it will also need to be timely and provide guidance for improvement
7. Will need to have the same evaluative criteria for all three samples. (Yes, they can be from different assessments, but must have the same rubric.)
8. Will need to reflect what your next steps for instruction will be for your students. This may reflect either whole class, subgroups, or individual instruction

Candidates have told me that next to the planning section of the Teaching Event, this was the second hardest and had the second longest commentaries…

Words of "Assessment" Wisdom from passing candidates:

- Be sure to have a strong pre-assessment to reflect back onto so that you can talk about data, what the students knew before and compare to their learning as a result of your lesson. I used a pre-assessment (Piaget conservation) that demonstrated developmental progress so I could rely on their levels when discussing their misconceptions, needs, etc.
- Go into depth about analyzing your students. Talk about patterns you saw.
- Make sure you have a clear rubric for every assessment associated with the PACT lessons and create data tables on how the class did as a whole as well as your subgroups. Doing this makes writing this section very easy since you can clearly see how your students performed. This will also help you when you start the reflection section.
- Giving an assessment where students have the opportunity to express their knowledge both written and verbally is a good idea because it gives you more to talk about. Create a rubric that assesses your objectives in the content and academic language.
- Keep all student work just in case you need to use a different assessment - Use the rubrics and ensure you have covered everything you needed to cover - Make sure you are assessing the students for the standard you are teaching - Start early, get feedback, ask questions
- Commit to an idea and run with it. Don't get analysis paralysis.
- Write rubrics for each assessment you give and make sure you have at least one every day of the learning segment.
- This section was a tough one. Don't slack on this one as it relates to the reflection section. The first time I completed the teaching event I failed both the assessment and reflection sections; that's how related they are!

CHAPTER 5
REFLECTING ON TEACHING & LEARNING

Readings

- Teaching Event Handbook pages 18 – 19
- Making Good Choices pages 18 – 20

Suggested Instructional Activities

- Peer-review reflection commentaries (see Appendix 7)
- I generally have two peer-review sessions, once for the reflection section and the second for the whole teaching event including academic language.
- Consider another citation session for candidates to include in their commentaries.

The Teaching Event Handbook describes this section as:

The Reflecting on Teaching & Learning Task describes what you learned from teaching the learning segment. It provides evidence of your ability to analyze your teaching and your students' learning to improve your teaching practice (Elementary Mathematics Teaching Event Candidate Handbook, 2013).

The Reflection rubrics are below and we will discuss them and the commentaries individually (Elementary Mathematics Rubrics, 2013).

EM 9: Monitoring Student Progress. How does the candidate monitor student learning and make appropriate adjustments in instruction during the learning segment?	EM 10: Reflecting on Learning. How does the candidate use research, theory, and reflections on teaching and learning to guide practice?
• Daily reflections indicate **monitoring of student progress toward meeting the standards/objectives for the learning segment.** • Adjustments to instruction are focused on **addressing some individual and collective learning needs**.	• Reflections on teaching practice are based on **sound knowledge of research and theory linked to knowledge of students** in the class. • Changes in teaching practice are based on reasonable assumptions about how student learning was affected by planning, instruction, or assessment decisions.

Writing the "Daily Reflections" and adjusting instruction (from planning and instruction sections)

If you did provide a rubric daily for each of the days in your learning segment, then you are probably well prepared to score well on this rubric. The rubric for EM 9 says that you will "monitor student progress toward meeting the standards/objectives…" (Elementary Mathematics Rubrics, 2013) What the rubric does **not** say is "how do you feel the students are doing with your lesson?" The commentaries, then, should be based on the data you collected for your assessments and what you wrote in the assessment commentaries. Again, think about beginning your paragraphs with "based on the data collected from the XX assessment…"

Rubric EM 10 (Elementary Mathematics Rubrics, 2013)

The first and second bullets relates to the research and theory that is linked to your knowledge of your students and should be connected to what you wrote in the planning section and your data findings in the assessment section. If you said that your struggling students did poorly in learning conceptual knowledge, then you'll need to have the research that supports this. We'll deal more on this with the commentaries.

The first prompt reads:

> *When you consider the content learning of your students and the development of their academic language, what do you think explains the learning or differences in learning that you observed during the learning segment? Cite relevant research or theory that explains what you observed. (See Planning Commentary, prompt # 2.) (TPEs 7, 8, 13)* (Teaching Event Handbook – Elementary Mathematics, 2013)

That prompt is asking you to comment on your findings from the assessment section. In order for you to explain what happened when you taught your learning segment you will need to provide the research that says that it will likely happen to your subgroup [*insert name of subgroup here*]. Your data observations came from your assessment section, and in this section you will let the assessor know that research in your content area supports your findings. This is not a "I think this happened because of…". This is a "this happened because Dr. So-and-So said it might happen." So get your foundational theoretical books out, and get to work!

The second prompt reads:

> *Based on your experience teaching this learning segment, what did you learn about your students as mathematics learners (e.g., easy/difficult concepts and skills, easy/difficult learning tasks, easy/difficult features of academic language, common misunderstandings)? Please cite specific evidence from previous Teaching Event tasks as well as **specific** research and theories that inform your analysis. (TPE 13)* (Teaching Event Handbook – Elementary Mathematics, 2013)

Again, you will discuss what happened in the learning segment, which researcher said it might happen, and the evidence to show that it did happen; namely your assessments. You will also need to cite research to support your findings.

The third prompt reads:

> *If you could go back and teach this learning segment again to the same group of students, what would you do differently in relation to planning, instruction, and assessment? How would the changes improve the learning of students with different needs and characteristics? (TPE 13)* (Teaching Event Handbook – Elementary Mathematics, 2013

Ok, almost done… That prompt is based on what you have previously written in both your assessment and reflection commentaries. You should not provide any new information here. What do you think "different needs and characteristics" means? Do you think it means that you will need to write to your subgroups? DUH.

Words of "Reflection" Wisdom from passing candidates:

- Do your daily reflections daily!!!!! This will help you when answering questions. Also print previous sections. This will help you when you need to refer back, especially when revisiting the quoting of the experts.
- There is always room for improvement. Don't be afraid to admit that you made mistakes and could have done better. Just be sure to have a plan for how to fix it and evidence or theorists to back that plan up
- Choose student samples that can help you reflect on what future changes you can make to the lesson that will better guide your future students. When talking about each student sample, do not address what the student does not know. It is your job as a teacher to try to understand what part of your planning did not guide the student to have the correct understanding. Reflect on how you will change the lesson, not on what the student were incapable of doing (as a class and as individuals, especially as groups).
- During the administration of the PACT unit or lesson series, write a teaching reflection for every day of teaching. Use these to help you complete the reflection section. - Do not wait until the last minute and try to make up a reflection. - Use the rubric and handbook!

I told you that this would be a big task: Aren't you glad you didn't procrastinate? I've included a few words of wisdom that speak to the whole process of teaching and writing for completing the Teaching Event. Good luck! I hope you have some very good news very soon.

General Words of Wisdom from passing candidates:

- PACT takes a ton of time, is stressful, and turned me into a miserable and tired maniac towards the end, but now that I have completed it, I feel so proud. Once I got my thoughts organized and did one step at a time it became a little less stressful; just very time consuming. Use Microsoft Word and make a separate folder for each section. That helped me a ton when working on it each night. Plug things in as you go along to keep your thoughts organized. It is a crazy semester, but the feeling you get when you press SUBMIT is amazing! Good luck!
- Reading the rubrics thoroughly will help structure responses to prompts. Incorporating key target words from rubrics (especially from the footnotes of the academic language rubrics) is a good idea. I personally color coded each task (pink = context, orange = planning, yellow = Instruction, green = assessment and blue = reflection) with post-its and flags. When I read a good quote in a book or something that was mentioned by professors or others, I flagged it with the assigned color post-it or highlighted it in the right color for coordinate with the task. I then put up a table and separated it into 5 color coded sections and placed papers/ rubric/ notes/ quotes etc. in piles. As I wrote each section, I grabbed it from the colored section and went through my collection. I think this really helped me visualize each task and how they interrelated.

- Be clear, concise, and thoroughly explain your thought processes during planning, teaching, and reflection, and your graders will be fair.
- Start early, think about a learning segment that has plenty of opportunity to incorporate student lead learning and strategies that you can reference to theory. Once you have your idea start planning, even if you will not be teaching the segment for another month. Once you get the commentary and the planning done everything else falls into place. Take your time and work on one question per section per day. Set small goals so you can meet them and feel like you accomplished something. Start pretend videotaping a couple weeks before you are going to teach your lesson to get the students use to the camera being there. Bribe students if you have to. Once you finish the PACT you will have a short lived period of relief, that relief only last for about a week before it turns into nervousness because you want to know how you did.
- Plan, plan, plan... You seriously already know all that you need. Just give yourself the time to show how much you've learned and the great potential that you have as a teacher.
- DO NOT Procrastinate. It is not something you will be able to complete in one day. It is stressful, a lot of work, time consuming, but if you are prepared, you will do just fine.

References

Brockman, G. (2006). What Factors Influence Achievement in Remedial Mathematics? Measures in Cognitive and Motivational Factors. Ann Arbor, MI: Proquest

California Department of Education. (2013). California Education Code: CELDT requirments. Retrieved on February 9, 2013 from http://www.cde.ca.gov/sp/el/rd/

Legislative Analyst's Office Report (2006). The Progress of English Learner Student: Legislative Analyst's Office Report. Retrieved on February 9, 2013 from http://www.google.com/url?sa=t&rct=j&q=&esrc=s&frm=1&source=web&cd=1&ved=0CCcQF jAA&url=http%3A%2F%2Fwww.lao.ca.gov%2F2006%2Feng_lrnr_updt%2Feng_lrnr_updt_01 2606.pdf&ei=hvbeUqDiDMqLqwHcpoCICg&usg=AFQjCNFZrOlsrAgqrVr7_ZhgThucLMjVd A&sig2=GwU0OtYszKPL5wsrmn7BTA&bvm=bv.59568121,d.aWM

McLead, G. B. (1993). Research on affect in mathematics education: A reconceptualization. *Handbook of Research on Mathematics Teaching and Learning.* London, CO: Macmillan Publishing.

Merrian-Webster. (2013). An Encyclopaedia Britannica Company. Retrieved on February 9, 2013 from http://www.merriam-webster.com/dictionary/discourse

PACT Consortium. (2013). Performance Assessment for California Teachers: Elementary Mathematics Rubrics. Retrieved on February 9, 2013 from www.pacttpa.org

PACT Consortium. (2013). Performance Assessment for California Teachers: Elementary Mathematics Teaching Event Handbook. Retrieved on February 9, 2013 from www.pacttpa.org

PACT Consortium. (2013). Performance Assessment for California Teachers: Science Teaching Event Handbook. Retrieved on October 9, 2015 from www.pacttpa.org

PACT Consortium. (2013). Performance Assessment for California Teachers: Science Rubrics. Retrieved on Retrieved on October 9, 2015 from www.pacttpa.org

Pintrich, P. R., & Schunk, D. H. (2002). *Motivation in Education: Theory, Research, and Applications, (2nd ed.).* Upper Saddle River, NJ: Pearson Education.

Schunk, D. H. (2004). Learning Theories: An Educational Perspective (4th ed). New Jersey: Pearson Prentice Hall Education, Inc.

Appendix 1 – Learning Segment Sample Template

Day 1	Day 2	Day 3
Standard	Standard	Standard
Objective	Objective	Objective
Engagement	Engagement	Engagement
Instruction	Instruction	Instruction
Application/Independent	Application/Independent	Application/Independent
Assessment	Assessment	Assessment
Materials	Materials	Materials

Appendix 2 – Task Validation Sample Template

Day	Learning Task/Activity	Purpose
Day 1		
Day 2		
Day 3		

Appendix 3 – CELDT Strategies Sample Template

CELDT Level	What Students Have	What Students Can Do	Strategies Teachers Can Use
1 – Beginning (Beginning English learners can communicate only in their primary language, they are very capable of higher level thinking skills)	• Their primary language • Minimal comprehension of English • Minimal verbal production in English with little or no receptive skills • One/two word responses that may be disconnected or memorized statements	• Nod and shake head to answer questions • Understand simple phrases • Speak a few words to communicate basic needs • Point to objects or print • Sort objects into categories • Pantomime • Draw pictures and label drawings and diagrams • Gesture to show understanding • Match objects or pictures • Give yes/no answers to simple questions • Reproduce what they hear, repeat and recite	
2 – Early Intermediate (Early intermediate students are still developing basic communication skills in receptive and productive language skills)	• One/two word responses • Limited proficiency to communicate ideas • Some comprehension of contextualized • Information • Developing receptive and productive language skills in English	• All of what student can do at the Beginning level, plus: • Understand and respond to simple school tasks • List and categorize • Repeat sentences, mimic intonation and phrasing and reproduce familiar phrases • Attempt to talk, making extensive pronunciation and grammatical errors • Generate and speak in simple sentences • Begin to acquire some grammatical elements • Read some basic vocabulary and write simple sentences • Give short answers to simple questions	
3 – Intermediate (Verbal communication skills are likely strong, but are not reliable indicators of their ability to	• Enough English proficiency to be understood • Ability to produce utterances with basic sentence structure (Subject +	• All of what students can do at the Beginning and Early Intermediate levels, plus: • Can speak, read and write in English on familiar topics • Describe people, places and events • Recall and state facts or tell simple	

		stories	
comprehend academic material)	Verb + Object or Phrase) • Able to identify and understand more concrete details • Ability to interact more with native speakers, but can make errors in speech • Good comprehension of contextualized information	• Define and explain some vocabulary • Make some errors in speech • Read and retell from a variety of texts with scaffolding from teacher • Begin to identify main ideas and details	
4 – Early Advanced (Students at this level need a strong emphasis on structured writing and continued vocabulary development)	• Good comprehension of information • Proficiency to communicate well verbally • Able to identify and summarize more concrete details and abstract concepts without modified instruction • Adequate vocabulary to achieve academically • Can write paragraphs and compositions	• Give opinions and reasons, draw comparisons, justify views and behaviors and summarize • Participate in increasingly complex tasks associated with school • Demonstrate ability to use higher order language, synthesize, analyze, evaluate, persuade and debate • Demonstrate both social and academic understanding of language • Identify main idea and details • Use expanded vocabulary • Engage in conversation and produce sequential narrative • Develop listening, speaking, reading and writing skills with increased comprehension	
5 – Advanced (Students at this level need ongoing development of background knowledge and must be challenged academically)	• Very good comprehension of information • Heightened proficiency to communicate well with various audiences. • Expanded vocabulary to achieve	• Comprehend and generate discussions and presentations in social as well as academic settings • Demonstrate fluency with content topics • Read and comprehend grade level texts • Respond to and use figurative language and idiomatic expressions appropriately • Organize and generate written compositions based on purpose, audience and subject matter	

	academically • Near native speech fluency	• Prepare and deliver presentations/reports across grade level content areas that use a variety of sources; include purpose, point of view, introduction, coherent transition and appropriate conclusions • Initiate and negotiate social conversation	

Appendix 4 – Scaffolding Terminology Sample

Scaffold	How does it support students' building of their understanding?	Some tasks that may be appropriate
Modeling	• Clarifies procedures through observing the action of others and can happen at various levels • Shows concrete examples of how a students' finished product may look	Warm ups Explicit modeling Routines Procedures
Bridging	• Provides a personal connection between the learner and the content • Taps into students' prior knowledge relevant to the class theme	KWL Think-Pair-Share Three-Step Interview Anticipatory Charts Brainstorming Framing Questions
Contextualization	• Provides a meaningful context that familiarizes new concepts	Use of manipulatives Video clips Realia Listening to music Oral Language Development Jigsaw
Schema Building	• Helps students establish the connections that exists between and across concepts that may otherwise appear unrelated • Explicitly organizing content knowledge	Compare/Contrast Matrix used as advanced organizer Fishbone used to diagram text Story Graph used to help skim through a text Concept Review Jigsaw Jigsaw Project

Metacognitive Development	• Supports students' internalization of strategies through a conscious focus on the implementation of plans of attack • Develops student autonomy through self-monitoring and self-assessment	Reciprocal Teaching KWL Charts Assessment Rubrics
Text Re-presentation	• Invites students to extend their understandings patterns, norms, and rules and apply them in new formats	Story Boards Collaborative dialog writing Oral Development Jigsaw Eye-witness accounts

Appendix 5 – Context for Learning Commentary Rubric Sample
Context for Learning Commentary Rubric

	Needs improvement	Novice	Adequate	Proficient
Academic Performance (Includes students' prior knowledge, key skills necessary to complete the learning segment for the teaching event, developmental levels, and other special educational needs)	Academic development lacks detail and insufficient indications that will influence your students' abilities in learning the content.	Academic development commentary is detail rich and contains a few (1 to 2) indications that will influence your students' abilities in learning the content.	Academic development commentary is detail rich and contains several (2 to 3) indications that will influence your students' abilities in learning the content.	Academic development commentary is detail rich and contains several (4 or more) indications that will influence your students' abilities in learning the content (gaps in knowledge, experience, and prior learning)
Language Development (Includes both conversational and academic language skills for each level with respect to reading, writing, listening and speaking)	Language development commentary is contains some of the following: * Attention to all levels of previously reported CELDT scores *Describes each level score the skills and language demands the students will need to complete the assignment and to participate in all classroom work, class activities, and homework. *Describes each level score what the students may struggle with to complete the assignment and to participate in the classroom activities.	Language development commentary is contains most of the following: * Attention to all levels of previously reported CELDT scores *Describes each level score the skills and language demands the students will need to complete the assignment and to participate in all classroom work, class activities, and homework. *Describes each level score what the students may struggle with to complete the assignment and to participate in the classroom activities.	Language development commentary is detail rich and contains the following: * Attention to all levels of previously reported CELDT scores *Describes each level score the skills and language demands the students will need to complete the assignment and to participate in all classroom work, class activities, and homework. *Describes each level score what the students may struggle with to complete the assignment and to participate in the classroom activities.	Language development commentary is detail rich and contains the following: * Attention to all levels of previously reported CELDT scores *Describes in detail for each level score the skills and language demands the students will need to complete the assignment and to participate in all classroom work, class activities, and homework. *Describes in detail for each level score what the students may struggle with to complete the assignment and to participate in the classroom activities.
Social Development (includes the	Social development commentary is lacking details that will enable	Social development commentary contains a few (2 to 3) indications	Social development commentary is detail rich and contains a few	Social development commentary is detail rich and contains

	Needs improvement	Novice	Adequate	Proficient
ability of students to express themselves in constructive ways, negotiate and solve problems, and the ability to get along with others)	the reader to understand the social development of the classroom	that will influence your students' abilities in learning the content (e.g., expressing themselves in constructive ways, negotiating and solving problems, ability to get along with others, ability/desire to participate in class discussions, etc.)	(2 to 3) indications that will influence your students' abilities in learning the content (e.g., expressing themselves in constructive ways, negotiating and solving problems, ability to get along with others, ability/desire to participate in class discussions, etc.)	several (4 or more) indications that will influence your students' abilities in learning the content (e.g., expressing themselves in constructive ways, negotiating and solving problems, ability to get along with others, ability/desire to participate in class discussions, etc.)
Family and community contexts (includes key factors related to cultural context, knowledge acquired outside of school, and home and community resources)	Family and community contexts lack key factors that affect students' ability to participate in classroom activities, complete class assignments, or complete homework (e.g., cultural knowledge, socio-economic background, access to technology, home/community resources.)	Family and community contexts contains a few (2 to 3) key factors that affect students' ability to participate in classroom activities, complete class assignments, or complete homework (e.g., cultural knowledge, socio-economic background, access to technology, home/community resources.)	Family and community contexts commentary is detail rich and contains a few (2 to 3) key factors that affect students' ability to participate in classroom activities, complete class assignments, or complete homework (e.g., cultural knowledge, socio-economic background, access to technology, home/community resources.)	Family and community contexts commentary is detail rich and contains several (4 or more) key factors that affect students' ability to participate in classroom activities, complete class assignments, or complete homework (e.g., cultural knowledge, socio-economic background, access to technology, home/community resources.)

Appendix 6 – Suggested Rubric Elements for Content Areas Sample

Suggested Rubric Elements	1	2	3	4
Art – Creative expression ELA – Facts HSS - Facts Math (EM & MAT) – Conceptual Music – Creative expression PE – Facts/conventions/skills Science – Concepts WL – Vocabulary/grammar				
Art – Artistic perception ELA – Understandings of text HSS – Concepts Math (EM & MAT) - Procedural Music – Artistic perception PE – Strategies and applications Science – Real world phenomena WL – Language function				
Art – Aesthetic valuing ELA – Interpretations of text HSS – Interpretations Math (EM & MAT) - Reasoning Music – Aesthetic valuing Science – Investigation skills WL – Text type				
Art – Understanding historical ELA – Response to text HSS – Judgments about… Music – Understanding historical… WL – Production and…				
Art – Understanding cultural Music – Understanding cultural				
Academic Language				

Appendix 7 – Checklist for Peer-review

Checklists for Art Teaching Events

Planning Instruction Commentary Checklist
(Minimum 4 double spaced pages*)

Lesson Plans	NA	LC	AC
Learning outcome described in lesson plan and is evident in both the instructional sequence and application sections of the lesson plan?			
Does the curriculum connection give information about where the lesson is placed in the unit plan?			
Includes a description of how the progression of learning tasks and assessments guides students to build **deep understandings** of the central focus of the learning segment.			
Includes a description of why the content of the learning segment is important for your particular students to learn (apart from being present in the school curriculum, student academic content standards, or ELD standards).			
Describes the engagement that activates prior knowledge.			
Includes a description of how the engagement motivate students to want to learn more?			
Does the engagement teach to the standard?			
Is the instructional sequence a "step-by-step" process?			
Is the instructional sequence clear and coherent?			
Does the instructional sequence teach to the standard?			
Are there clear connections among creative expression, artistic perception, aesthetic valuing and understanding art in historical and cultural context?			
Includes a description of key learning tasks in the plan that build on each other to support students' creative expression and artistic perception as well as their understanding of aesthetic valuing and visual art in historical and cultural context, and the development of related academic language.			
Includes a description of language demands of the learning and assessment tasks are likely to be challenging for the candidates' students.			
Includes a description of the learning and assessment tasks in the candidates' plan to support students in meeting their language demands.			
Includes a description of the instructional strategies tailored to address a variety of specific student learning needs? i.e., are the instructional strategies tailored to meet the needs of the student population in which the lesson occurs?			
Includes a description of how your knowledge of the candidates' students informed the lesson plans, such as the choice of text materials used in lessons using student learning or experiences as a resource, or structuring new learning to take advantage of specific student strengths.			
Includes a description of how the knowledge of the candidates' students informed how groups were formed or structured using student learning or experiences as a resource, or structuring new learning to take advantage of specific student strengths.			
Includes a description of how the progression of learning tasks include scaffolding			

or other forms of structured support to provide access to grade-level standards/objectives.			
Includes a description of how the strategies for the learning tasks are tailored to address a variety of specific student learning needs.			
Are all materials and resources listed?			
Are the accommodations for individual learners included in the lesson plan?			
Are all worksheets included in the lesson plan?			
Assessments			
Do the assessments provide opportunities for students to learn what is assessed and are relative to students' skill and developmental level?			
Includes a description of how the candidate allowed students to show some depth of understanding or skill with respect to the standards/objectives.			
Includes a description of how the candidate assessed both productive and receptive modalities to monitor students understanding AND are designed, modified, or adapted to allow students with special needs opportunities to demonstrate understandings and skills relative to the standards/objectives.			

NA= Not addressed

LC = Limited coverage;

AC = Adequate coverage

* Recommended page requirement is listed in the Teaching Event

Instructional Video and Commentary Checklist
(Minimum 4 double-spaced pages*)

Video	NA	LC	AC
Do the strategies for intellectual engagement seen in the video clip(s) offer structured opportunities for students to actively improve their own understanding of creative expression, artistic perception, aesthetic valuing and the historical and cultural context of visual art?			
Do the strategies reflect attention to students' characteristics, learning needs, and/or language needs?			
Are the strategies used explicit and clearly reflect attention to students with diverse characteristics, learning needs, and/or language needs?			
Does the teacher monitor student understanding by eliciting student responses that require thinking?			
Is it evident that the teacher builds upon student responses as a guide to improve students' understanding of creative expression, artistic perception, aesthetic valuing and the historical and cultural context of visual art? (Would be especially evident in student inaccuracies and misunderstandings, but also to deepen students' understanding of the content)			
Is the teacher able to recognize incomplete progress from the students toward the standards/objectives for this lesson?			
If incomplete progress toward the standards/objectives of this lesson (inaccuracies and misunderstandings) are evident, does the teacher use this opportunity to identify and redirect instruction such that students are able to master the instructional objective?			
Does the teacher elicit students' responses and explanations of thinking to further the understanding of the students? (deepen students' understanding of the content)			
Do any inaccuracies exist that inhibit a clear understanding for students?			
Commentary			
Is the reader informed about what happened immediately prior to the video clip?			
Are routines (from the classroom) stated to inform the reader about students' learning strategies, language needs, diversity issues, developmental needs, etc. that are important to the function of the class and curriculum?			
Does the author discuss the teacher's ability to further the knowledge and skills, and engagement of students' intellectual understanding of creative expression, artistic perception, aesthetic valuing and the historical and cultural context of visual art? In relation to the needs of all of the students?			
Are there at least 2 different descriptions of the use of language supports for struggling and English learners?			
Are there at least 2 examples of student dialog that relates to monitoring student learning during the video clip?			
Is there a reflection on student learning for the lesson?			
Does the student learning reflection address teacher's subsequent planning and teaching?			
Does the student learning reflection address successes as well as missed opportunities?			

NA= Not addressed
LC = Limited coverage
AC = Adequate coverage
* **Recommended page requirement is listed in the Teaching Event**

Assessment Commentary
(Minimum 4 double spaced pages*)

	NA	LC	AC
Are there at least 3 student samples included with the commentary? At least one sample should be from an English Language Learner.			
Do the student samples contain constructive feedback from the instructor? Does the feedback provide the student with guidance to improve their work?			
Are the student work samples labeled Student A, B, and C?			
Are rubrics or grading criteria included for all formal assessments?			
Are the assessments a measure of proficiency for the standards/objectives?			
Does the candidate include a summary of students' prior knowledge of the content and their individual learning strengths and challenges?			
Does the candidate include a conclusion about the students' learning during the learning segment? Does the conclusion cite specific evidence from the work samples?			
Does the candidate include a conclusion about the students' learning during the learning segment? Does the conclusion cite specific evidence from the work samples?			
Daily journal entries – Is there a description of how the art lesson provide students with opportunities to learn what was being taught? (Based on evidence from assessments only)			
Daily journal entries – Is there a description of how the art lesson allowed students to show some depth of understanding or skill with respect to the standards/objectives? (Based on evidence from assessments only)			
Daily journal entries – Is there a description from the lesson you taught that identifies the next steps to focus on improving student performance through targeted support to individuals and groups to address specific misunderstandings or needs? (Based on evidence from assessments only)			
Daily journal entries – Are the next steps listed above include one or more of the following: feedback to students, specific instructional activities, re-teaching for support, and extended learning activities. (Based on evidence from assessments only)			
Daily journal entries – Are the next steps listed above targeted to support individuals and groups and specific to students' needs and misunderstandings? (Based on evidence from assessments only)			
Daily journal entries – Is there a description of what adjustments to instruction should be made to focus on individual and collective needs? (Based on evidence from assessments only)			
Daily journal entries – Is there a description from the analysis of student work, of any specific patterns for individuals or subgroups in addition to the whole class? Is there a description of what are they? Is there a description of why you think these patterns exist? (Based on evidence from assessments only)			
Daily journal entries – Is the identified next steps (from analysis of student work) incorporated into the next day lesson plans? (adjustments to instruction should be made to focus on individual and collective needs)			
Daily journal entries – Is the identified next steps (from analysis of student work) addressed in the following day's journal entry?			
Daily journal entries – Do the next steps demonstrate a strong understanding of both the content and language standards/objectives of individual students and/or subgroups?			
Is there a summary of student learning across the whole class relative to your evaluative criteria?			

NA= Not addressed
LC = Limited coverage
AC = Adequate coverage
* Recommended page requirement is listed in the Teaching Event

Reflection Commentary
(Minimum 4 double spaced pages*)

	NA	LC	AC
Are daily reflections included that monitor student progress toward meeting the standards/objective for the learning segment?			
Do the daily reflections address adjustments to instruction that focus on the individual and collective learning needs of the students?			
Are the adjustments to instruction implemented? (Should be evident in the next daily reflection)			
Describe the results of student learning including an evaluation of teacher effectiveness by recognizing your strengths and weaknesses.			
Describe what you would do differently if you taught this lesson again and why. On what evidence do you base your changes to the lesson?			
Are the reflections on teaching practice based on sound knowledge of research and theory linked to knowledge of students in the class?			
Are the reflections on teaching practice based on sound knowledge of research and theory linked to knowledge of the content?			
Are specific strategies noted that change the teaching practice to strategically improve the individual and collective understanding of the students toward the standards/objectives?			
Relevant research or theory is cited			

NA= Not addressed
LC = Limited coverage
AC = Adequate coverage
* Recommended page requirement is listed in the Teaching Event

Checklists for English Teaching Events
English Planning Instruction Commentary Checklist

Lesson Plans	NA	LC	AC
Learning outcome is described in lesson plan and is evident in both the instructional sequence and application sections of the lesson plan?			
Describes how the curriculum connection provides information about where the lesson is placed in the unit plan?			
Describes a progression of learning tasks and assessments guides students to build deep understandings of the central focus of the learning segment.			
Describes why the content of the learning segment is important for your particular students to learn.			
Provides the title, author, and a short discussion of salient features of the text(s) used during the learning segment. (What would a reviewer who is unfamiliar with the text(s) need to know about them in order to understand your instruction? These might include such things as the genre, theme, plot, or linguistic features.)			
Describes the engagement that activates prior knowledge.			
Describes how the engagement motivates students to want to learn more?			
Describes how the engagement teaches to the standard?			
Is the instructional sequence a "step-by-step" process?			
Is the instructional sequence clear and coherent?			
Does the instructional sequence teach to the standard?			
Describes how the learning tasks build on each other to support student learning of how to understand, interpret, and respond to complex text, and to develop related academic language.			
Are the instructional strategies well integrated into the engagement and instructional sequence?			
Does the choice of strategies in the learning segment draw upon students' prior learning as well as experiential backgrounds or interests to help students reach the learning segments standards/objectives?			
Are the instructional strategies tailored to address a variety of specific student learning needs? i.e., are the instructional strategies tailored to meet the needs of the student population in which the lesson occurs?			
Do the instructional strategies, scaffolding or other forms of structured support allow students access to grade-level standards/objectives?			
Describes language demands of the learning and assessment tasks are likely to be challenging for your students.			
Describes how the learning tasks and the set of assessment tasks focus on multiple dimensions of English-language arts learning through clear connections among facts, understandings of the text, interpretations of the text, and response to the text.			
Does the application practice what is taught in the instructional sequence?			
Does the application provide ample practice for students?			
Are all materials and resources listed?			
Do the formative assessment strategies provide students with ample feedback during the lesson?			
Assessments access both productive and receptive modalities to monitor student understanding			

Are the accommodations for individual learners included in the lesson plan?			
Are all worksheets included in the lesson plan?			
Assessments			
Describes how the assessments provide opportunities for students to learn what is assessed and are relative to students' skill and developmental level?			
Describes how the assessments allow students to show some depth of understanding or skill with respect to the standards/objectives?			
Describes how the collection of assessments from your plan allows you to evaluate your students' learning of specific student standards/objectives			
Describes how the assessments are deliberately modified, adapted, and/or designed to allow students with special needs opportunities to demonstrate understandings and skills relative to the standards/objectives? (English learners, GATE, students with IEPs)			

NA = Not addressed   LC = Limited coverage   AC = Adequate coverage

English Instructional Video and Commentary Checklist

Video	NA	LC	AC
Do the strategies for intellectual engagement seen in the video clip(s) offer structured opportunities for students to actively evaluate accounts or interpretations about a historical event or social science phenomenon and to defend their own judgments?			
Do the strategies reflect attention to students' characteristics, learning needs, and/or language needs?			
Are the strategies used explicit and clearly reflect attention to students with diverse characteristics, learning needs, and/or language needs?			
Is it evident that the teacher builds upon student responses as a guide to improve students' knowledge and skills and engage them intellectually in understanding, interpreting, and/or responding to a complex text?			
Is the teacher able to recognize incomplete progress from the students toward the standards/objectives for this lesson?			
If incomplete progress toward the standards/objectives of this lesson (inaccuracies and misunderstandings) is evident, does the teacher use this opportunity to identify and redirect instruction such that students are able to critically evaluate/interpret the instructional objective?			
Does the teacher elicit students' responses and explanations of their evaluations or interpretations and uses these explanations to further the understanding of all students?			
Do any inaccuracies exist that inhibit a clear understanding for students?			
Commentary			
Describes how the reader is informed about what happened immediately prior to the video clip?			
Describes how the routines (from the classroom) are stated to inform the reader about students' learning strategies, language needs, diversity issues, developmental needs, etc. that are important to the function of the class and curriculum?			
Describes how the teacher is able to eliciting students' responses that require explanations of student thinking and uses these explanations to further the understanding of all students?			
Are there at least 2 different descriptions of the use of language supports for struggling and English learners?			
Describes and provides examples of language supports used in the clips to help your students understand the content and/or academic language central to the lessons.			
Are there at least 2 examples of student dialog that relates to monitoring student learning during the video clip?			
Is there a reflection on student learning for the lesson?			
Does the student learning reflection address teacher's subsequent planning and teaching?			
Does the student learning reflection address successes as well as missed opportunities?			

NA = Not addressed   LC = Limited coverage   AC = Adequate coverage

English Assessment Commentary

	NA	LC	AC
Does the candidate identify specific standards/objectives measured by the assessment chosen for analysis?			
Are there at least 3 student samples included with the commentary? At least one sample should be from an English Language Learner.			
Do the student samples contain constructive feedback from the instructor? Does the feedback provide the student with guidance to improve their work?			
Does the author discuss summary of students' prior knowledge of the content and their individual learning strengths and challenges?			
Does the candidate include a conclusion about the students' learning during the learning segment? Does the conclusion cite specific evidence from the work samples?			
Are the student work samples labeled Student A, B, and C?			
Are rubrics or grading criteria included for all formal assessments?			
Does the evaluative criteria's include understanding the author's use of imagery, or use of evidence from the text to support an interpretation?			
Are the assessments a measure of proficiency for the standards/objectives?			
Daily journal entries – Is there a description of how the learning segment provided students with opportunities to learn what was being taught? (Based on evidence from assessments only)			
Daily journal entries – Is there a description of how the learning segment allowed students to show some depth of understanding or skill with respect to the standards/objectives? (Based on evidence from assessments only)			
Daily journal entries – Is there a description from the learning segment you taught that identifies the next steps to focus on improving student performance through targeted support to individuals and groups to address specific misunderstandings or needs? (Based on evidence from assessments only)			
Daily journal entries – Are the next steps listed above include one or more of the following: feedback to students, specific instructional activities, re-teaching for support, and extended learning activities. (Based on evidence from assessments only)			
Daily journal entries – Are the next steps listed above targeted to support individuals and groups and specific to students' needs and misunderstandings? (Based on evidence from assessments only)			
Daily journal entries – Describes how the next steps demonstrate a strong understanding of both the identified content and language standards/objectives and of individual students and/or subgroups.			
Daily journal entries – Is there a description of what adjustments to instruction should be made to focus on individual and collective needs? (Based on evidence from assessments only)			
Daily journal entries – Is there a description from the analysis of student work, of any specific patterns for individuals or subgroups in addition to the whole class? Is there a description of what are they? Is there a description of why you think these patterns exist? (Based on evidence from assessments only)			
Daily journal entries – Is the identified next steps (from analysis of student work) incorporated into the next day lesson plans? (adjustments to instruction should be made to focus on individual and collective needs)			
Daily journal entries – Is the identified next steps (from analysis of student work) addressed in the following day's journal entry?			
Daily journal entries – Do the next steps demonstrate a strong understanding of both the content and language standards/objectives of individual students and/or subgroups?			
Is there a summary of student learning across the whole class relative to your evaluative criteria?			

NA = Not addressed   LC = Limited coverage   AC = Adequate coverage

English Reflection Commentary

	NA	LC	AC
Are daily reflections included that monitor student progress toward meeting the standards/objective for the learning segment?			
Do the daily reflections address adjustments to instruction that focus on the individual and collective learning needs of the students?			
Describes how the adjustments to instruction focus on deepening key skills and understandings related to understanding, interpreting, or responding to complex features of a text.			
Are the adjustments to instruction implemented? (Should be evident in the next daily reflection)			
Describe the results of student learning including an evaluation of teacher effectiveness by recognizing your strengths and weaknesses.			
Describe what you would do differently if you taught this lesson again and why. On what evidence do you base your changes to the lesson?			
Are the reflections on teaching practice based on sound knowledge of research and theory linked to knowledge of students in the class?			
Are the reflections on teaching practice based on sound knowledge of research and theory linked to knowledge of the content?			
Are specific strategies noted change the teaching practice to strategically improve the individual and collective understanding of the students toward the standards/objectives?			
Relevant research or theory is cited			

NA = Not addressed   LC = Limited coverage   AC = Adequate coverage

Checklists for History Social Studies Teaching Events
HSS Planning Instruction Commentary Checklist

Lesson Plans	NA	LC	AC
Learning outcome is described in lesson plan and is evident in both the instructional sequence and application sections of the lesson plan?			
Describes how the curriculum connection provides information about where the lesson is placed in the unit plan?			
Describes a progression of learning tasks and assessments guides students to build deep understandings of the central focus of the learning segment			
Describes the engagement that activates prior knowledge.			
Describes how the engagement motivates students to want to learn more?			
Describes how the engagement teaches to the standard?			
Is the instructional sequence a "step-by-step" process?			
Is the instructional sequence clear and coherent?			
Does the instructional sequence teach to the standard?			
Describes how the learning tasks and assessment encourage students to use facts concepts, and interpretations to make and explain judgments about a significant historical event or social science phenomenon?"			
Are the instructional strategies well integrated into the engagement and instructional sequence?			
Does the learning segment draw upon students' prior learning as well as experiential backgrounds or interests to help students reach the learning segments standards/objectives?			
Are the instructional strategies tailored to address a variety of specific student learning needs? i.e., are the instructional strategies tailored to meet the needs of the student population in which the lesson occurs?			
Do the instructional strategies, scaffolding or other forms of structured support allow students access to grade-level standards/objectives?			
Does the application practice what is taught in the instructional sequence?			
Does the application provide ample practice for students?			
Are all materials and resources listed?			
Do the formative assessment strategies provide students with ample feedback during the lesson?			
Are the accommodations for individual learners included in the lesson plan?			
Are all worksheets included in the lesson plan?			
Assessments			
Describes how the assessments provide opportunities for students to learn what is assessed and are relative to students' skill and developmental level?			
Describes how the assessments allow students to show some depth of understanding or skill with respect to the standards/objectives?			
Describes how the assessments access both productive (speaking/writing) and receptive (listening/reading) modalities to monitor student understanding?			
Describes how the assessments are deliberately modified, adapted, and/or designed to allow students with special needs opportunities to demonstrate understandings and skills relative to the standards/objectives?			

NA = Not addressed   LC = Limited Coverage   AC = Adequate Coverage

HSS Instructional Video and Commentary Checklist

Video	NA	LC	AC
Do the strategies for intellectual engagement seen in the video clip(s) offer structured opportunities for students to actively evaluate accounts or interpretations about a historical event or social science phenomenon and to defend their own judgments?			
Do the strategies reflect attention to students' characteristics, learning needs, and/or language needs?			
Are the strategies used explicit and clearly reflect attention to students with diverse characteristics, learning needs, and/or language needs?			
Does the teacher monitor student understanding by eliciting student responses that require mathematical reasoning or problem solving strategies?			
Is it evident that the teacher builds upon student responses as a guide to improve students' understanding by eliciting students' responses that require evaluations of history/social science accounts or evaluations of interpretations?			
Is the teacher able to recognize incomplete progress from the students toward the standards/objectives for this lesson?			
If incomplete progress toward the standards/objectives of this lesson (inaccuracies and misunderstandings) is evident, does the teacher use this opportunity to identify and redirect instruction such that students are able to critically evaluate/interpret the instructional objective?			
Does the teacher elicit students' responses and explanations of their evaluations or interpretations and uses these explanations to further the understanding of all students?			
Do any inaccuracies exist that inhibit a clear understanding for students?			
Commentary			
Describes how the reader is informed about what happened immediately prior to the video clip?			
Describes how the routines (from the classroom) are stated to inform the reader about students' learning strategies, language needs, diversity issues, developmental needs, etc. that are important to the function of the class and curriculum?			
Describes how the teacher's is able to eliciting students' responses that require evaluations of history/social science accounts or evaluations of interpretations? In relation to the needs of all of the students?			
Are there at least 2 different descriptions of the use of language supports for struggling and English learners?			
Are there at least 2 examples of student dialog that relates to monitoring student learning during the video clip?			
Is there a reflection on student learning for the lesson?			
Does the student learning reflection address teacher's subsequent planning and teaching?			
Does the student learning reflection address successes as well as missed opportunities?			

NA = Not addressed   LC = Limited coverage   AC = Adequate coverage

HSS Assessment Commentary

	NA	LC	AC
Does the candidate identify specific standards/objectives measured by the assessment chosen for analysis?			
Are there at least 3 student samples included with the commentary? At least one sample should be from an English Language Learner.			
Do the student samples contain constructive feedback from the instructor? Does the feedback provide the student with guidance to improve their work?			
Does the author discuss summary of students' prior knowledge of the content and their individual learning strengths and challenges?			
Does the candidate include a conclusion about the students' learning during the learning segment? Does the conclusion cite specific evidence from the work samples?			
Are the student work samples labeled Student A, B, and C?			
Are rubrics or grading criteria included for all formal assessments?			
Does the evaluative criteria's include correct identification of key historical facts or people, supportive evidence for an argument or interpretation, or appropriate application of specific concepts?			
Are the assessments a measure of proficiency for the standards/objectives?			
Daily journal entries – Is there a description of how the learning segment provided students with opportunities to learn what was being taught? (Based on evidence from assessments only)			
Daily journal entries – Is there a description of how the learning segment allowed students to show some depth of understanding or skill with respect to the standards/objectives? (Based on evidence from assessments only)			
Daily journal entries – Is there a description from the learning segment you taught that identifies the next steps to focus on improving student performance through targeted support to individuals and groups to address specific misunderstandings or needs? (Based on evidence from assessments only)			
Daily journal entries – Are the next steps listed above include one or more of the following: feedback to students, specific instructional activities, re-teaching for support, and extended learning activities. (Based on evidence from assessments only)			
Daily journal entries – Are the next steps listed above targeted to support individuals and groups and specific to students' needs and misunderstandings? (Based on evidence from assessments only)			
Daily journal entries – Is there a description of what adjustments to instruction should be made to focus on individual and collective needs? (Based on evidence from assessments only)			
Daily journal entries – Is there a description from the analysis of student work, of any specific patterns for individuals or subgroups in addition to the whole class? Is there a description of what are they? Is there a description of why you think these patterns exist? (Based on evidence from assessments only)			
Daily journal entries – Is the identified next steps (from analysis of student work) incorporated into the next day lesson plans? (adjustments to instruction should be made to focus on individual and collective needs)			
Daily journal entries – Is the identified next steps (from analysis of student work) addressed in the following day's journal entry?			
Daily journal entries – Do the next steps demonstrate a strong understanding of both the content and language standards/objectives of individual students and/or subgroups?			
Is there a summary of student learning across the whole class relative to your evaluative criteria?			

NA = Not addressed   LC = Limited coverage   AC = Adequate coverage

HSS Reflection Commentary

	NA	LC	AC
Are daily reflections included that monitor student progress toward meeting the standards/objective for the learning segment?			
Do the daily reflections address adjustments to instruction that focus on the individual and collective learning needs of the students?			
Are the adjustments to instruction implemented? (Should be evident in the next daily reflection)			
Describe the results of student learning including an evaluation of teacher effectiveness by recognizing your strengths and weaknesses.			
Describe what you would do differently if you taught this lesson again and why. On what evidence do you base your changes to the lesson?			
Are the reflections on teaching practice based on sound knowledge of research and theory linked to knowledge of students in the class?			
Are the reflections on teaching practice based on sound knowledge of research and theory linked to knowledge of the content?			
Are specific strategies noted change the teaching practice to strategically improve the individual and collective understanding of the students toward the standards/objectives?			
Do the specific strategies help to deepen key skills and understandings related to using facts, concepts, and interpretations to make and explain judgments about a significant historical event or social science phenomenon?			
Relevant research or theory is cited			

NA = Not addressed   LC = Limited coverage   AC = Adequate coverage

Checklists for Mathematics Teaching Events

Mathematics Planning Instruction Commentary

Lesson Plans	NA	LC	AC
Learning outcome described in lesson plan and is evident in both the instructional sequence and application sections of the lesson plan?			
Does the curriculum connection give information about where the lesson is placed in the unit plan?			
MS & Math – Content type includes both conceptual knowledge and procedural knowledge?			
A progression of learning tasks and assessments guides students to build deep understandings of the central focus of the learning segment			
Describes the engagement that activates prior knowledge.			
Does the engagement motivate students to want to learn more?			
Does the engagement teach to the standard?			
Is the instructional sequence a "step-by-step" process?			
Is the instructional sequence clear and coherent?			
Does the instructional sequence teach to the standard?			
Are there clear connections among the computations/procedures, concepts and reasoning/problem solving?			
Are the instructional strategies well integrated into the engagement and instructional sequence?			
Are the instructional strategies tailored to address a variety of specific student learning needs? i.e., are the instructional strategies tailored to meet the needs of the student population in which the lesson occurs?			
Does the application practice what is taught in the instructional sequence?			
Does the application provide ample practice for students?			
Are all materials and resources listed?			
Do formative assessment strategies provide students with ample feedback during the lesson?			
Are the accommodations for individual learners included in the lesson plan?			
Are all worksheets included in the lesson plan?			
Assessments			
Do the assessments provide opportunities for students to learn what is assessed and are relative to students' skill and developmental level?			
Do the assessments allow students to show some depth of understanding or skill with respect to the standards/objectives?			
Do the assessments access both productive (speaking/writing) and receptive (listening/reading) modalities to monitor student understanding?			
Are the assessments deliberately modified, adapted, and/or designed to allow students with special needs opportunities to demonstrate understandings and skills relative to the standards/objectives?			

NA = Not addressed   LC = Limited coverage   AC = Adequate coverage

Math Instructional Video and Commentary Checklist

Video	NA	LC	AC
Do the strategies for intellectual engagement seen in the video clip(s) offer structured opportunities for students to actively develop their own understanding of mathematical concepts and discourse.			
Do the strategies reflect attention to students' characteristics, learning needs, and/or language needs?			
Are the strategies used explicit and clearly reflect attention to students with diverse characteristics, learning needs, and/or language needs?			
Does the teacher monitor student understanding by eliciting student responses that require mathematical reasoning or problem solving strategies?			
Is it evident that the teacher builds upon student responses as a guide to improve students' understanding of mathematical concepts and discourse? (Would be especially evident in student inaccuracies and misunderstandings, but also to deepen students' understanding of the content)			
Is the teacher able to recognize incomplete progress from the students toward the standards/objectives for this lesson?			
If incomplete progress toward the standards/objectives of this lesson (inaccuracies and misunderstandings) are evident, does the teacher use this opportunity to identify and redirect instruction such that students are able to master the instructional objective?			
Does the teacher elicit students' responses and explanations of their reasoning and problem solving strategies used to further the understanding of the students? (deepen students' understanding of the content)			
Do any inaccuracies exist that inhibit a clear understanding for students?			
Commentary			
Is the reader informed about what happened immediately prior to the video clip?			
Are routines (from the classroom) stated to inform the reader about students' learning strategies, language needs, diversity issues, developmental needs, etc. that are important to the function of the class and curriculum?			
Does the author discuss the teacher's ability to further the knowledge and skills, and engagement of students' intellectual understanding of the concepts and mathematical discourse? In relation to the needs of all of the students?			
Are there at least 2 different descriptions of the use of language supports for struggling and English learners?			
Are there at least 2 examples of student dialog that relates to monitoring student learning during the video clip?			
Is there a reflection on student learning for the lesson?			
Does the student learning reflection address teacher's subsequent planning and teaching?			
Does the student learning reflection address successes as well as missed opportunities?			

NA = Not addressed   LC = Limited coverage   AC = Adequate coverage

Mathematics Assessment Commentary

	NA	LC	AC
Are there at least 3 student samples included with the commentary? At least one sample should be from an English Language Learner.			
Do the student samples contain constructive feedback from the instructor? Does the feedback provide the student with guidance to improve their work?			
Are the student work samples labeled Student A, B, and C?			
Are rubrics or grading criteria included for all formal assessments?			
Are the assessments a measure of proficiency for the standards/objectives?			
Does the candidate include a summary of students' prior knowledge of the content and their individual learning strengths and challenges?			
Does the candidate include a conclusion about the students' learning during the learning segment? Does the conclusion cite specific evidence from the work samples?			
Does the candidate include a conclusion about the students' learning during the learning segment? Does the conclusion cite specific evidence from the work samples?			
Daily journal entries – Is there a description of how the math lesson provide students with opportunities to learn what was being taught? (Based on evidence from assessments only)			
Daily journal entries – Is there a description of how the math lesson allowed students to show some depth of understanding or skill with respect to the standards/objectives? (Based on evidence from assessments only)			
Daily journal entries – Is there a description from the lesson you taught that identifies the next steps to focus on improving student performance through targeted support to individuals and groups to address specific misunderstandings or needs? (Based on evidence from assessments only)			
Daily journal entries – Are the next steps listed above include one or more of the following: feedback to students, specific instructional activities, re-teaching for support, and extended learning activities. (Based on evidence from assessments only)			
Daily journal entries – Are the next steps listed above targeted to support individuals and groups and specific to students' needs and misunderstandings? (Based on evidence from assessments only)			
Daily journal entries – Is there a description of what adjustments to instruction should be made to focus on individual and collective needs? (Based on evidence from assessments only)			
Is there a description from the analysis of student work, of any specific patterns for individuals or subgroups in addition to the whole class? Is there a description of what are they? Is there a description of why you think these patterns exist? (Based on evidence from assessments only)			
Is the identified next steps (from analysis of student work) incorporated into the next day lesson plans? (adjustments to instruction should be made to focus on individual and collective needs)			
Daily journal entries – Is the identified next steps (from analysis of student work)			

addressed in the following day's journal entry?			
Do the next steps demonstrate a strong understanding of both the content and language standards/objectives of individual students and/or subgroups?			
Is there a summary of student learning across the whole class relative to your evaluative criteria?			

NA = Not addressed   LC = Limited coverage   AC = Adequate coverage

Mathematics Reflection Commentary

	NA	LC	AC
Are daily reflections included that monitor student progress toward meeting the standards/objective for the learning segment?			
Do the daily reflections address adjustments to instruction that focus on the individual and collective learning needs of the students?			
Are the adjustments to instruction implemented? (Should be evident in the next daily reflection)			
Describe the results of student learning including an evaluation of teacher effectiveness by recognizing your strengths and weaknesses.			
Describe what you would do differently if you taught this lesson again and why. On what evidence do you base your changes to the lesson?			
Are the reflections on teaching practice based on sound knowledge of research and theory linked to knowledge of students in the class?			
Are the reflections on teaching practice based on your assessment of student's work and linked to knowledge of the content?			
Are specific strategies noted that change the teaching practice to strategically improve the individual and collective understanding of the students toward the standards/objectives?			
Relevant research or theory is cited			

NA = Not addressed   LC = Limited coverage   AC = Adequate coverage

Checklists for Music Teaching Events

Planning Instruction Commentary Checklist
(Minimum 4 double spaced pages*)

Lesson Plans	NA	LC	AC
Learning outcome described in lesson plan and is evident in both the instructional sequence and application sections of the lesson plan?			
Does the curriculum connection give information about where the lesson is placed in the unit plan?			
Includes a description of how the progression of learning tasks and assessments guides students to build **deep understandings** of the central focus of the learning segment.			
Includes a description of why the content of the learning segment is important for your particular students to learn (apart from being present in the school curriculum, student academic content standards, or ELD standards).			
Describes the engagement that activates prior knowledge.			
Includes a description of how the engagement motivate students to want to learn more?			
Does the engagement teach to the standard?			
Is the instructional sequence a "step-by-step" process?			
Is the instructional sequence clear and coherent?			
Does the instructional sequence teach to the standard?			
Are there clear connections among the computations/procedures, concepts and reasoning/problem solving?			
Includes a description of key learning tasks in the plan that build on each other to support students' creative expression and artistic perception as well as their understanding of aesthetic valuing and understanding music in historical and cultural context, and the development of related academic language.			
Includes a description of language demands of the learning and assessment tasks are likely to be challenging for the candidates' students.			
Includes a description of the learning and assessment tasks in the candidates' plan to support students in meeting their language demands.			
Includes a description of the instructional strategies tailored to address a variety of specific student learning needs? i.e., are the instructional strategies tailored to meet the needs of the student population in which the lesson occurs?			
Includes a description of how your knowledge of the candidates' students informed the lesson plans, such as the choice of text materials used in lessons using student learning or experiences as a resource, or structuring new learning to take advantage of specific student strengths.			
Includes a description of how the knowledge of the candidates' students informed how groups were formed or structured using student learning or experiences as a resource, or structuring new learning to take advantage of specific student strengths.			
Includes a description of how the progression of learning tasks include scaffolding or other forms of structured support to provide access to grade-level standards/objectives.			

Includes a description of how the strategies for the learning tasks are tailored to address a variety of specific student learning needs.			
Are all materials and resources listed?			
Are the accommodations for individual learners included in the lesson plan?			
Are all worksheets included in the lesson plan?			
Assessments			
Do the assessments provide opportunities for students to learn what is assessed and are relative to students' skill and developmental level?			
Includes a description of how the candidate allowed students to show some depth of understanding or skill with respect to the standards/objectives.			
Includes a description of how the candidate assessed both productive and receptive modalities to monitor students understanding AND are designed, modified, or adapted to allow students with special needs opportunities to demonstrate understandings and skills relative to the standards/objectives.			

NA= Not addressed
LC = Limited coverage
AC = Adequate coverage
* Recommended page requirement is listed in the Teaching Event

Music Instructional Video and Commentary Checklist
(Minimum 4 double-spaced pages*)

Video	NA	LC	AC
Do the strategies for intellectual engagement seen in the video clip(s) offer structured opportunities for students to **actively develop and apply specific musical skills and strategies to perform, create, analyze, describe or understand music**			
Do the strategies reflect attention to students' characteristics, learning needs, and/or language needs?			
Are the strategies used explicit and clearly reflect attention to students with diverse characteristics, learning needs, and/or language needs?			
Does the teacher monitor student understanding by eliciting verbal or musical responses that require thinking?			
Is it evident that the teacher builds upon student responses as a guide to improve students' understanding of musical elements and discourse? (Would be especially evident in student inaccuracies and misunderstandings, but also to deepen students' understanding of the content)			
Is the teacher able to recognize incomplete progress from the students toward the standards/objectives for this lesson?			
If incomplete progress toward the standards/objectives of this lesson (inaccuracies and misunderstandings) are evident, does the teacher use this opportunity to identify and redirect instruction such that students are able to master the instructional objective?			
Does the teacher elicit students' responses and explanations of their reasoning and musical understanding to further the understanding of the students? (deepen students' understanding of the content)			
Do any inaccuracies exist that inhibit a clear understanding for students?			
Commentary			
Is the reader informed about what happened immediately prior to the video clip?			
Are routines (from the classroom) stated to inform the reader about students' learning strategies, language needs, diversity issues, developmental needs, etc. that are important to the function of the class and curriculum?			
Does the author discuss the teacher's ability to further the knowledge and skills, and engagement of students' intellectual understanding of musical concepts/elements and discourse? In relation to the needs of all of the students?			
Are there at least 2 different descriptions of the use of language supports for struggling and English learners?			
Are there at least 2 examples of student dialog that relates to monitoring student learning during the video clip?			
Is there a reflection on student learning for the lesson?			
Does the student learning reflection address teacher's subsequent planning and teaching?			
Does the student learning reflection address successes as well as missed opportunities?			

    NA= Not addressed
    LC = Limited coverage
    AC = Adequate coverage
 * Recommended page requirement is listed in the Teaching Event

Assessment Commentary
(Minimum 4 double spaced pages*)

	NA	LC	AC
Are there at least 3 student samples included with the commentary? At least one sample should be from an English Language Learner OR is there evidence from the video clip (evaluative performance is clearly seen) that represents students' individual performance that clearly document performances to identify patterns in skill and/or understanding?			
Do the student samples/clips contain constructive feedback from the instructor? Does the feedback provide the student with guidance to improve their work?			
Are the student work samples labeled Student A, B, and C?			
Are rubrics or grading criteria included for all formal assessments?			
Are the assessments a measure of proficiency for the standards/objectives?			
Does the candidate include a summary of students' prior knowledge of the content and their individual learning strengths and challenges?			
Does the candidate include a conclusion about the students' learning during the learning segment? Does the conclusion cite specific evidence from the work samples?			
Does the candidate include a conclusion about the students' learning during the learning segment? Does the conclusion cite specific evidence from the work samples?			
Daily journal entries – Is there a description of how the music lesson provide students with opportunities to learn what was being taught? (Based on evidence from assessments only)			
Daily journal entries – Is there a description of how the music lesson allowed students to show some depth of understanding or skill with respect to the standards/objectives? (Based on evidence from assessments only)			
Daily journal entries – Is there a description from the lesson you taught that identifies the next steps to focus on improving student performance through targeted support to individuals and groups to address specific misunderstandings or needs? (Based on evidence from assessments only)			
Daily journal entries – Are the next steps listed above include one or more of the following: feedback to students, specific instructional activities, re-teaching for support, and extended learning activities. (Based on evidence from assessments only)			
Daily journal entries – Are the next steps listed above targeted to support individuals and groups and specific to students' needs and misunderstandings? (Based on evidence from assessments only)			
Daily journal entries – Is there a description of what adjustments to instruction should be made to focus on individual and collective needs? (Based on evidence from assessments only)			
Daily journal entries – Is there a description from the analysis of student work, of any specific patterns for individuals or subgroups in addition to the whole class? Is there a description of what are they? Is there a description of why you think these patterns exist? (Based on evidence from assessments only)			
Daily journal entries – Is the identified next steps (from analysis of student work) incorporated into the next day lesson plans? (adjustments to instruction should be made to focus on individual and collective needs)			
Daily journal entries – Is the identified next steps (from analysis of student work) addressed in the following day's journal entry?			
Daily journal entries – Do the next steps demonstrate a strong understanding of both the content and language standards/objectives of individual students and/or subgroups?			
Is there a summary of student learning across the whole class relative to your evaluative criteria?			

NA= **Not addressed**
LC = **Limited coverage**
AC = **Adequate coverage**

Reflection Commentary
(Minimum 4 double spaced pages*)

	NA	LC	AC
Are daily reflections included that monitor student progress toward meeting the standards/objective for the learning segment?			
Do the daily reflections address adjustments to instruction that focus on the individual and collective learning needs of the students?			
Are the adjustments to instruction implemented? (Should be evident in the next daily reflection)			
Describe the results of student learning including an evaluation of teacher effectiveness by recognizing your strengths and weaknesses.			
Describe what you would do differently if you taught this lesson again and why. On what evidence do you base your changes to the lesson?			
Are the reflections on teaching practice based on sound knowledge of research and theory linked to knowledge of students in the class?			
Are the reflections on teaching practice based on sound knowledge of research and theory linked to knowledge of the content?			
Are specific strategies noted that change the teaching practice to strategically improve the individual and collective understanding of the students toward the standards/objectives?			
Relevant research or theory is cited			

NA= Not addressed

LC = Limited coverage

AC = Adequate coverage

* **Recommended page requirement is listed in the Teaching Event**

Physical Education Checklist

PE Planning Instruction Commentary Checklist

Lesson Plans	NA	LC	AC
Learning outcome is described in lesson plan and is evident in both the instructional sequence and application sections of the lesson plan?			
Includes a description of how the curriculum connection provides information about where the lesson is placed in the unit plan?			
Includes a description of a progression of learning tasks and assessments guides students to build deep understandings of the central focus of the learning segment			
Includes a description of the engagement that activates prior knowledge.			
Includes a description of how the engagement motivates students to want to learn more/participate?			
Includes PEC standards or ELD standards.			
Includes a description of how the engagement teaches to the standard?			
Includes a description of how the instructional sequence a "step-by-step" process?			
Is the instructional sequence is clear and coherent?			
Does the instructional sequence teach to the standard?			
Includes a description of why the content of the learning segment is important for the candidate's students to learn.			
The central focus of the learning segment is evident throughout the planning section.			
Includes a description of how the key learning tasks build on each other to develop students' knowledge and competency in motor skills, movement patterns, and strategies.			
Includes a description of how the learning segment supports students' academic language as it relates to the learning task.			
Does the learning segment draw upon students' prior learning as well as experiential backgrounds or interests to help students reach the learning segments standards/objectives?			
Are the instructional strategies tailored to address a variety of specific student learning needs? i.e., are the instructional strategies tailored to meet the needs of the student population in which the lesson occurs?			
Includes a description of how the choice of instructional strategies help to inform the candidate of lesson planning by using student learning or experiences as a resource, or structuring new learning to take advantage of specific student strengths.			
Includes a description of choice of text or other materials (if applicable) to take advantage of specific student strengths.			
Includes a description of how groups were formed or structured to take advantage of specific student strengths.			
Includes a description of how the set of learning tasks make a clear connection between facts/conventions/skills and strategies/applications.			
Do the instructional strategies help build student learning across the learning segment?			

Does the application practice what is taught in the instructional sequence?			
Does the application provide ample practice for students?			
Are all materials and resources listed?			
Do the formative assessment strategies provide students with ample feedback during the lesson?			
Are the accommodations for individual learners included in the lesson plan?			
Includes a description of any language demands of learning tasks are likely to be challenging for the students.			
Includes a description of how the specific features of the learning tasks support students in meeting language demands.			
Includes a description of how the learning tasks help build deep understandings of the central focus of the learning segment.			
Assessments			
Includes a description of how the assessments provide opportunities for students to learn what is assessed and are relative to students' skill and developmental level?			
Includes a description of how the assessments allow the candidate to evaluate students' learning of specific student standards/objectives.			
Includes a description of any language demands from the assessment tasks are likely to be challenging for the students.			
Includes a description of how the specific features of the assessment tasks support students in meeting language demands.			
Includes a description of how the assessments are deliberately modified, adapted, and/or designed to allow students with special needs opportunities to demonstrate understandings and skills relative to the PEC standards/objectives?			
Includes a description of how the set of assessment tasks make a clear connection between facts/conventions/skills and strategies/applications.			
Includes a description of how the assessments tasks help build deep understandings of the central focus of the learning segment.			

NA = Not addressed   LC = Limited coverage   AC = Adequate coverage

PE Instructional Video and Commentary Checklist

Video	NA	LC	AC
Are the strategies for intellectual engagement seen in the video clip(s) offer structured opportunities for students to actively enhance their own knowledge of and competency in motor skills and movement patterns?			
Do the strategies reflect attention to students' characteristics, learning needs, and/or language needs?			
Are the strategies used explicit and clearly reflect attention to students with diverse characteristics, learning needs, and/or language needs?			
Does the candidate monitor student understanding by eliciting student responses that require thinking or strategic movement?			
Is it evident that the teacher builds upon student input as a guide to improve students' knowledge of and competency in motor skills and movement patterns?			
Is the teacher able to recognize incomplete progress from the students toward the standards/objectives for this lesson?			
If incomplete progress toward the standards/objectives of this lesson (inaccuracies and misunderstandings) is evident, does the teacher use this opportunity to identify and redirect instruction such that students are able to critically evaluate/interpret the instructional objective?			
Does the teacher elicit students' responses and explanations of their evaluations or interpretations and uses these explanations to further the understanding of all students?			
Do any inaccuracies exist that inhibit a clear understanding for students?			
Commentary			
Includes a description of how the reader is informed about what happened immediately prior to the video clip?			
Includes a description of how the routines (from the classroom) are stated to inform the reader about students' learning strategies, language needs, diversity issues, developmental needs, etc. that are important to the function of the class and curriculum?			
Includes a description of how the candidate is able to further students' knowledge, skills, and strategies related to the physical activity and engage them intellectually.			
Includes a description of at least 2 different support strategies to help students to understand the content and/or academic language central to the lesson.			
Includes a description of how support strategies (at least 2) as seen in the video clips, supported students' academic language.			
There are at least 2 examples of student dialog that relates to monitoring student learning during the video clip that indicate their progress toward accomplishing the lesson's learning objectives.			
Is there a reflection on student learning for the lesson?			
Does the student learning reflection address teacher's subsequent planning and teaching?			
Does the student learning reflection address successes as well as missed opportunities?			

NA = Not addressed   LC = Limited coverage   AC = Adequate coverage

PE Assessment Commentary

	NA	LC	AC
Does the candidate identify specific standards/objectives measured by the assessment chosen for analysis?			
Are there at least 3 student samples included with the commentary? At least one sample should be from an English Language Learner OR is there evidence from the video clip (evaluative performance is clearly seen) that represents students' individual performance that clearly document performances to identify patterns in skill and/or understanding?			
Do the student samples contain constructive feedback from the instructor? Does the feedback provide the student with guidance to improve their work?			
Includes a description of how the evaluative criteria measure student proficiency for all goals/objectives. Categories of evaluative criteria (or rubric) include knowledge of rules for a sport and their function, technical proficiency in a movement pattern.			
Includes a description of how the written assessment of student learning across the whole class is relative to the evaluative criteria (or rubric) OR how a physical activity describes your expectations for the performance according to your evaluative criteria or provides a rubric and indicates which characteristics of the selected performance are typical of almost all the students in the class, most students in the class, some students in the class, etc. or are unique to the individual.			
Includes a description of summarizing the results in narrative and/or graphic form.			
Does the candidate include a conclusion about the students' learning during the learning segment? Does the conclusion cite specific evidence from the work samples?			
Are the student work samples labeled Student A, B, and C?			
Are rubrics or grading criteria included for all formal assessments?			
Includes a description of how the 3 student work samples were collected and describes their prior knowledge of the content/activity and their individual learning strengths and challenges.			
Includes a description of how the assessments analyze student motor skills and movement patterns in relation to the PEC standards/objectives?			
Daily journal entries – Is there a description of how the learning segment provided students with opportunities to learn what was being taught? (Based on evidence from assessments only)			
Daily journal entries – Is there a description of how the learning segment allowed students to show some depth of understanding or skill with respect to the standards/objectives? (Based on evidence from assessments only)			
Daily journal entries – Is there a description from the learning segment you taught that identifies the next steps to focus on improving student performance through targeted support to individuals and groups to address specific misunderstandings or needs? (Based on evidence from assessments only)			
Daily journal entries – Are the next steps listed above include one or more of the following: feedback to students, specific instructional activities, re-teaching for support, and extended learning activities. (Based on evidence from assessments only)			
Daily journal entries – Are the next steps listed above targeted to support individuals and groups and specific to students' needs and misunderstandings? (Based on evidence from assessments only)			
Daily journal entries – Is there a description of what adjustments to instruction should be made to focus on individual and collective needs? (Based on evidence from assessments			

only)			
Daily journal entries – Is there a description from the analysis of student work, of any specific patterns for individuals or subgroups in addition to the whole class? Is there a description of what are they? Is there a description of why you think these patterns exist? (Based on evidence from assessments only)			
Daily journal entries – Is the identified next steps (from analysis of student work) incorporated into the next day lesson plans? (adjustments to instruction should be made to focus on individual and collective needs)			
Daily journal entries – Is the identified next steps (from analysis of student work) addressed in the following day's journal entry?			
Daily journal entries – Do the next steps demonstrate a strong understanding of both the content and language standards/objectives of individual students and/or subgroups?			

NA = Not addressed   LC = Limited coverage   AC = Adequate coverage

PE Reflection Commentary

	NA	LC	AC
Are daily reflections included that monitor student progress toward meeting the PEC standards/objective for the learning segment?			
Describes how the daily reflections address adjustments to instruction that focus on the individual and collective learning needs of the students?			
Are the adjustments to instruction implemented? (Should be evident in the next daily reflection)			
Includes a description of how the candidate considered the content and skill learning of the students and the development of their academic language.			
Includes a description explaining the learning or differences in learning that was observed during the learning segment.			
Includes a description of the candidate's impression of what they learned about their students as physical education learners and has cited specific evidence from previous Teaching Event tasks as well as specific research and theories that inform the analysis.			
Includes a description of how the reflections on teaching practice based on sound knowledge of research and theory linked to knowledge of students in the class?			
Includes a description of how specific strategies noted, change the teaching practice to strategically improve the individual and collective understanding of the students toward the standards/objectives.			
Includes a description of how the specific strategies help to deepen knowledge and competency in motor skills and movement patterns.			
Includes a description of what the candidate would do differently in relation to planning, instruction, and assessment if the learning segment could be taught again.			
Includes a description of what the candidate would do differently in relation to planning, instruction, and assessment if the learning segment could be taught again to improve the learning of the students with different needs and characteristics.			
Relevant research or theory is cited			

NA = Not addressed   LC = Limited coverage   AC = Adequate coverage

Checklists for Science Teaching Events

Science Planning Instruction Commentary Checklist

Lesson Plans	NA	LC	AC
Learning outcome is described in lesson plan and is evident in both the instructional sequence and application sections of the lesson plan			
Does the curriculum connection give information about where the lesson is placed in the unit plan?			
A progression of learning tasks and assessments guides students to build deep understandings of the central focus of the learning segment			
Describes the engagement that activates prior knowledge of students			
Does the engagement motivate students to want to learn more?			
Does the engagement teach to the standard?			
Is the instructional sequence a "step-by-step" process?			
Is the instructional sequence clear and coherent?			
Does the instructional sequence teach to the standard?			
Are there clear connections among the learning tasks and the set of assessment tasks that focus on multiple dimensions of science learning through clear connections among science concepts, real world phenomena, and investigation/experimentation skills?			
Are the instructional strategies well integrated into the engagement and instructional sequence?			
Does the learning segment draw upon students' prior learning as well as experiential backgrounds or interests to help students reach the learning segments standards/objectives?			
Are the instructional strategies tailored to address a variety of specific student learning needs? i.e., are the instructional strategies tailored to meet the needs of the student population in which the lesson occurs?			
Do the instructional strategies, scaffolding or other forms of structured support allow students access to grade-level standards/objectives?			
Does the application practice what is taught in the instructional sequence?			
Does the application provide ample practice for students?			
Are all materials and resources listed?			
Do the formative assessment strategies provide students with ample feedback during the lesson?			
Are the accommodations for individual learners included in the lesson plan?			
Are all worksheets included in the lesson plan?			
Assessments			
Do the assessments provide opportunities for students to learn what is assessed and are relative to students' skill and developmental level?			
Do the assessments allow students to show some depth of understanding or skill with respect to the standards/objectives?			
Do the assessments access both productive (speaking/writing) and receptive (listening/reading) modalities to monitor student understanding?			
Are the assessments deliberately modified, adapted, and/or designed to allow students with special needs opportunities to demonstrate understandings and skills relative to the standards/objectives?			

NA = Not addressed   LC = Limited coverage   AC = Adequate coverage

Science Instructional Video and Commentary Checklist

Video	NA	LC	AC
Do the strategies for intellectual engagement seen in the video clip(s) offer structured opportunities for students to actively collect, analyze, and interpret scientific data?			
Do the strategies reflect attention to students' characteristics, learning needs, and/or language needs?			
Are the strategies used explicit and clearly reflect attention to students with diverse characteristics, learning needs, and/or language needs?			
Does the teacher monitor student understanding by eliciting student responses that require mathematical reasoning or problem solving strategies?			
Is it evident that the teacher builds upon student responses as a guide to improve students' understanding by eliciting students' responses that require structured opportunities for students to actively collect, analyze, and interpret scientific data?			
Is the teacher able to recognize incomplete progress from the students toward the standards/objectives for this lesson?			
If incomplete progress toward the standards/objectives of this lesson (inaccuracies and misunderstandings) is evident, does the teacher use this opportunity to identify and redirect instruction such that students are able to critically evaluate/interpret the instructional objective?			
Do any inaccuracies exist that inhibit a clear understanding for students?			
Commentary			
Is the reader informed about what happened immediately prior to the video clip?			
Are routines (from the classroom) stated to inform the reader about students' learning strategies, language needs, diversity issues, developmental needs, etc. that are important to the function of the class and curriculum?			
Does the author discuss the teacher's ability to eliciting students' responses that further students' knowledge and skills and engage them intellectually while collecting, analyzing, and interpreting data from a scientific inquiry?			
Does the author provide examples of both general strategies to address the needs of all students and strategies to address specific individual needs?			
Are there at least 2 different descriptions of the use of language supports for struggling and English learners?			
Are there at least 2 examples of student dialog that relates to monitoring student learning during the video clip?			
Is there a reflection on student learning for the lesson?			
Does the student learning reflection address teacher's subsequent planning and teaching?			
Does the student learning reflection address successes as well as missed opportunities?			

NA = Not addressed   LC = Limited coverage   AC = Adequate coverage

Science Assessment Commentary

	NA	LC	AC
Does the candidate identify specific standards/objectives measured by the assessment chosen for analysis?			
Are there at least 3 work student samples included with the commentary? At least one sample should be from an English Language Learner.			
Does the candidate include a summary of students' prior knowledge of the content and their individual learning strengths and challenges?			
Does the candidate include a conclusion about the students' learning during the learning segment? Does the conclusion cite specific evidence from the work samples?			
Are the student work samples labeled Student A, B, and C?			
Are rubrics or grading criteria included for all formal assessments?			
Does the evaluative criteria's include an understanding of a particular science concept, the relationship between two concepts, or the fit between evidence and conclusions?			
Are the assessments a measure of proficiency for the standards/objectives?			
Daily journal entries – Is there a description of how the learning segment provided students with opportunities to learn what was being taught? (Based on evidence from assessments only)			
Daily journal entries – Is there a description of how the learning segment allowed students to show some depth of understanding or skill with respect to the standards/objectives? (Based on evidence from assessments only)			
Daily journal entries – Are there a description from the learning segment you taught that identifies the next steps to focus on improving student performance through targeted support to individuals and groups to address specific misunderstandings or needs? (Based on evidence from assessments only)			
Daily journal entries – Are the next steps listed above include one or more of the following: feedback to students, specific instructional activities, re-teaching for support, and extended learning activities. (Based on evidence from assessments only)			
Daily journal entries – Are the next steps listed above targeted to support individuals and groups and specific to students' needs and misunderstandings? (Based on evidence from assessments only)			
Daily journal entries – Is there a description of what adjustments to instruction should be made to focus on individual and collective needs? (Based on evidence from assessments only)			
Daily journal entries – Is there a description from the analysis of student work, of any specific patterns for individuals or subgroups in addition to the whole class? Is there a description of what are they? Is there a description of why you think these patterns exist? (Based on evidence from assessments only)			
Is the identified next steps (from analysis of student work) incorporated into the next day lesson plans? (adjustments to instruction should be made to focus on individual and collective needs)			
Is the identified next steps (from analysis of student work) addressed in the following day's journal entry?			
Do the next steps demonstrate a strong understanding of both the content and language standards/objectives of individual students and/or subgroups?			
Is there a summary of student learning across the whole class relative to your evaluative criteria?			

NA = Not addressed   LC = Limited coverage   AC = Adequate coverage

Science Reflection Commentary

	NA	LC	AC
Are daily reflections included that monitor student progress toward meeting the standards/objective for the learning segment?			
Do the daily reflections address adjustments to instruction that focus on the individual and collective learning needs of the students?			
Are the adjustments to instruction implemented? (Should be evident in the next daily reflection)			
Describe the results of student learning including an evaluation of teacher effectiveness by recognizing your strengths and weaknesses.			
Describe what you would do differently if you taught this lesson again and why. On what evidence do you base your changes to the lesson?			
Are the reflections on teaching practice based on sound knowledge of research and theory linked to knowledge of students in the class?			
Are the reflections on teaching practice based on your assessment data collection and linked to knowledge of the content?			
Are specific strategies noted, change the teaching practice to strategically improve the individual and collective understanding of the students toward the standards/objectives?			
Do the specific strategies help to deepen key skills and understandings related to using facts, concepts, and interpretations to make and explain judgments about a significant historical event or social science phenomenon?			
Relevant research or theory is cited			

NA = Not addressed   LC = Limited coverage   AC = Adequate coverage

Checklists for World Language Teaching Events

World Language Planning Instruction Commentary

Lesson Plans	NA	LC	AC
Learning outcome is described in lesson plan and is evident in both the instructional sequence and application sections of the lesson plan?			
Does the curriculum connection give information about where the lesson is placed in the unit plan?			
A progression of learning tasks and assessments guides students to build deep understandings of the central focus of the learning segment			
Apart from the present school curriculum, the Language Learning Continuum, or ELD standards, does the author discuss why the content of the learning segment is important for the students to learn?			
Does the author include a description of the language tasks, including assessments, that are likely to be challenging for the students?			
Des ribes how the tasks plan to support students in developing communicative proficiency in the target language relative to your language objectives?			
Describes the engagement that activates prior knowledge.			
Does the engagement motivate students to want to learn more?			
Does the engagement teach to the standard?			
Is the instructional sequence a "step-by-step" process?			
Is the instructional sequence clear and coherent?			
Does the instructional sequence teach to the standard?			
Are the instructional strategies well integrated into the engagement and instructional sequence?			
Does the learning segment draw upon students' prior learning as well as experiential backgrounds or interests to help students reach the learning segments standards/objectives?			
Are the instructional strategies tailored to address a variety of specific student learning needs? i.e., are the instructional strategies tailored to meet the needs of the student population in which the lesson occurs?			
Do the instructional strategies provide students access to the curriculum and allow them to demonstrate their acquisition of the target language in cultural context?			
Do the instructional strategies, scaffolding or other forms of structured support allow students access to grade-level standards/objectives?			
Does the application practice what is taught in the instructional sequence?			
Does the application provide ample practice for students?			
Are all materials and resources listed?			
Do the formative assessment strategies provide students with ample feedback during the lesson?			
Are the accommodations for individual learners included in the lesson plan?			
Are all worksheets included in the lesson plan?			
Is there a reference list for materials used in the lesson plan?			
Planning Commentary and/or Lesson Plans			
Describes key language tasks in your plans build on each other to support students; development of communicative proficiency (both productive and receptive) relative to the LLC and related language objectives, and their familiarity with cultures that use that			

	NA	LC	AC
language?			
Describe what demands of the language tasks, including assessments, are likely to be challenging for your students.			
Do the assessments provide opportunities for students to learn what is assessed and are relative to students' skill and developmental level?			
Do the assessments allow students to show some depth of understanding or skill with respect to the standards/objectives?			
Do the assessments access both productive (speaking/writing) and receptive (listening/reading) modalities to monitor student understanding?			
Are the assessments deliberately modified, adapted, and/or designed to allow students with special needs opportunities to demonstrate understandings and skills relative to the standards/objectives?			
Describes how the collection of assessments from your plan allows you to evaluate your students' acquisition of the target language in cultural context relative to the expected learning outcomes in the LLC and language objective that you have selected.			
Describes any instructional strategies you have planned for your students who have identified educational needs (e.g., English learners, GATE students, students with IEPs). Explains how these features of your language tasks, including assessments, will provide students access to the curriculum and allow them to demonstrate their acquisition of the target language in cultural context.			

NA= Not addressed   LC = Limited coverage   AC = Adequate coverage

World Language Instructional Video and Commentary

Video	NA	LC	AC
Do the strategies seen in the clips for engaging students in language production/comprehension offer structured opportunities for students to actively communicate in the target language in culturally appropriate ways?			
Do the strategies reflect attention to students' characteristics, learning needs, and/or language needs?			
Are the strategies used explicit and clearly reflect attention to students with diverse characteristics, learning needs, and/or language needs?			
Does the teacher monitor students' language production/comprehension by eliciting students' use of the target language and evaluating it in ways that go beyond the correct usage of grammar and vocabulary to address communicative proficiency in cultural context?			
Is it evident that the teacher builds upon student responses as a guide to improve students' abilities to communicate in the target language in culturally appropriate ways?			
Is the teacher able to recognize incomplete progress from the students toward the standards/objectives for this lesson?			
If incomplete progress toward the standards/objectives of this lesson (inaccuracies and misunderstandings) is evident, does the teacher use this opportunity to identify and redirect instruction such that students are able to critically evaluate/interpret the instructional objective?			
Do any inaccuracies exist that inhibit a clear understanding for students?			
Does the teacher response to help students learn strategies for improving their automaticity and fluency?			
Commentary			
Is the reader informed about what happened immediately prior to the video clip that is important to know in order to understand and interpret the interactions between and among you and your students?			
Are routines (from the classroom) stated to inform the reader about students' learning strategies, language needs, diversity issues, developmental needs, etc. that are important to the function of the class and curriculum?			
Describe how the engagement of students was able to further develop their communicative proficiency with respect to specific language functions and/or text types?			
Describes any language supports used in the clips to help your students produce and/or comprehend the vocabulary, targeted language functions, and/or text types and understand the cultural context central to the lessons?			
Does the author provide examples of both general strategies to address the needs of all students and strategies to address specific individual needs?			
Are the strategies used to monitor student communicative proficiency and understanding of the cultural context discussed from the video clip?			
Are there at least 2 examples of student dialog that relates to monitoring student learning during the video clip?			
Is there a reflection on student learning for the lesson?			
Does the student learning reflection address teacher's subsequent planning and teaching?			
Does the student learning reflection address successes as well as missed opportunities?			

NA = Not addressed   LC = Limited coverage   AC = Adequate coverage

World Language Assessment Commentary

	NA	LC	AC
Describes specific standards/objectives measured by the assessment chosen for analysis?			
Describes the evaluative criteria measure for student proficiency on the expected learning outcomes of the LLC and/or language objectives.			
Describes the evaluative criteria including listening comprehension, use of language functions, or understanding of cultural conventions.			
Are there at least 3 student samples included with the commentary?			
Do the 3 student samples together represent what students generally were able to produce/comprehend and what a number of students were still struggling with. At least one of these students should be an English learner who is a heritage speaker with oral but not written language proficiency in the target language or for whom the target language is not the primary language.			
Describes students' prior knowledge of the content and their individual learning strengths and challenges? (Whole class – may be displayed in table or chart form)			
Describes a conclusion about the students' learning during the learning segment? Does the conclusion cite specific evidence from the work samples?			
Are the student work samples labeled Student A, B, and C?			
Are rubrics or grading criteria included for all formal assessments?			
Describes patterns in automaticity, fluency, and accuracy to analyze students' communicative proficiency in relation to aspects of the LLC/objectives.			
Describes students' use of strategies for comprehension/production. Analysis is clear and detailed.			
Describes the evaluative criteria including in terms of students' communicative proficiency relative to the expected learning outcomes in the LLC and/or language objectives including both strengths and, if relevant, any needs (including a need for greater challenge) that were apparent for some or most students. (Evidence is cited to support analysis from the three student work samples selected)			
Are the assessments a measure of proficiency for the standards/objectives?			
Daily journal entries – Is there a description of how the learning segment provided students with opportunities to learn what was being taught? (Based on evidence from assessments only)			
Daily journal entries – Is there a description of how the learning segment allowed students to show some depth of understanding or skill with respect to the standards/objectives? (Based on evidence from assessments only)			
Daily journal entries – Is there a description from the learning segment you taught that identifies the next steps to focus on improving student performance through targeted support to individuals and groups to address specific misunderstandings or needs? (Based on evidence from assessments only)			
Daily journal entries – Are the next steps listed above include one or more of the following: feedback to students, specific instructional activities, re-teaching for support, and extended learning activities. (Based on evidence from assessments only)			
Daily journal entries – Are the next steps listed above targeted to support individuals and groups and specific to students' needs and misunderstandings? (Based on evidence from assessments only)			
Daily journal entries – Describes how next steps demonstrate a strong understanding of both the identified communication objectives and of individual students and/or subgroups.			
Daily journal entries – Is there a description of what adjustments to instruction should be made to focus on individual and collective needs? (Based on evidence from assessments			

only)			
Daily journal entries – Is there a description from the analysis of student work, of any specific patterns for individuals or subgroups in addition to the whole class? Is there a description of what are they? Is there a description of why you think these patterns exist? (Based on evidence from assessments only)			
Daily journal entries – Is the identified next steps (from analysis of student work) incorporated into the next day lesson plans? (adjustments to instruction should be made to focus on individual and collective needs)			
Daily journal entries – Is the identified next steps (from analysis of student work) addressed in the following day's journal entry?			
Daily journal entries – Do the next steps demonstrate a strong understanding of both the content and language standards/objectives of individual students and/or subgroups?			
Is there a summary of student learning across the whole class relative to your evaluative criteria?			

NA = Not addressed   LC = Limited coverage   **AC = Adequate coverage**

World Language Reflection Commentary

	NA	LC	AC
Are daily reflections included that monitor student progress toward meeting the standards/objective for the learning segment?			
Do the daily reflections address adjustments to instruction that focus on the individual and collective learning needs of the students?			
Are the adjustments to instruction implemented? (Should be evident in the next daily reflection)			
Describes the level of acquisition or differences in levels that you observed during the learning segment in terms of students' communicative proficiency in the target language.			
Describes what the candidate learned about students as learners of the target language in a cultural context.			
Describe the results of student learning including an evaluation of teacher effectiveness by recognizing your strengths and weaknesses.			
Describe what you would do differently if you taught this lesson again and why. On what evidence do you base your changes to the lesson?			
Are the reflections on teaching practice based on sound knowledge of research and theory linked to knowledge of students in the class?			
Are the reflections on teaching practice based on sound knowledge of research and theory linked to knowledge of the content?			
Are specific strategies noted, change the teaching practice to strategically improve the individual and collective understanding of the students toward the standards/objectives?			
Do the specific strategies help to deepen key skills and understandings related to using facts, concepts, and interpretations to make and explain judgments about a significant historical event or social science phenomenon?			
Relevant research or theory is cited			

NA= Not addressed   **LC = Limited coverage**   **AC = Adequate coverage**

Appendix 8 – Framework Examples

Cognitive Development	Piaget	Four Stages of Cognitive Development
		• Infancy: Sensorimotor Stage (approx. 0 to 2)
		  ○ Assimilation, accommodation, equilibration, disequilibrium, sensorimotor, object permanence
		• Preoperational Stage (approx. 2 to 7)
		  ○ Goal directed actions, operations, preoperational, semiotic functions
		• Concrete-Operational Stage (approx. 7 to 11)
		  ○ Reversible thinking, conservation, decentering, egocentric, concrete operations, identity, compensation, classification, reversibility, seriation
		• Formal Operations (approx. 11 to adult)

	Vygotsky	Sociocultural theory – emphasizes that children learn through interactions, shared activities and internal processes. • Co-constructed process – people learn through social interaction to create understanding or to problem solve with more knowledgeable/capable peers/persons • Zone of Proximal Development – the mastery of a task if the person is supported with help • Private speech
Self, Social and Moral Development	Bronfenbrenner	Bioecological Model – a series of nested microsystems describing the social development of people • Mesosystem, Exosystem, Macrosystem • Describes family structures, parenting styles, cultures in the home, cliques, friendships, peers, bullies
	Erikson	Psychosocial Development Stages – describes an individual's emotional needs and identity within a social environment (the how and where do I fit in?) • Basic trust vs. basic mistrust • Autonomy vs. shame • Initiative vs. guilt • Industry vs. inferiority • Identity vs. role confusion • Intimacy vs. isolation • Generativity vs. stagnation • Ego integrity vs. despair
	Kohlberg	Moral Development and Reasoning • Preconventional Moral Reasoning – judgement is based on other's rules and personal needs • Conventional Moral Reasoning – judgement is based on other's approval, family expectations, cultural values, laws and loyalties • Postconventional Moral Reasoning – judgement is based on "universal ethical" principles •

Learner Differences and Learning Needs & Cognitive View of Learning	Gardner	Multiple Intelligences – intelligences are biologically based and are viewed as separate abilities • Linguistic/verbal • Musical • Spatial • Logical/mathematical • Bodily/kinesthetic • Interpersonal • Intrapersonal • Naturalist
	Information Processing	Theory explains how the human mind takes in, stores and recalls information • Executive Control • Sensory memory – focusing attention • Working memory • Long-term memory – declarative and procedural knowledge retention
Cognitive and Social Constructivism	Vygotsky	Learning is a social interaction using cultural tools and activities in an environment conducive to learning
	Constructivism	• Knowledge is socially constructed • Learning takes place in complex, realistic, and relative learning environments • Social negotiation and shared responsibility • Support with multiple perspectives and representations • Inquiry and problem-based learning • Collaboration and cooperation
Social Cognitive Learning and Motivation	Bandura	Triarchic Reciprocal Causality – 3 influences that play a role in learning, person, environment and behavioral • Self-efficacy • Modeling • Mastery vs. performance • Enactive vs. vicarious experiences • Social persuasion • Affect and learned helplessness • Self-regulated learning (Zimmerman) • Anxiety
	Motivation	• Intrinsic motivation • Extrinsic motivation • Behavioral approach (Skinner) • Humanistic approach (Maslow) • Cognitive approach (Weiner) • Social cognitive approach (Bandura)
	Maslow	Hierarchy of needs • Basic • Psychological • Self-fulfillment
	Self-Determination	We need to feel competent and comfortable in our interactions in the world with a sense of control over our lives as well as connected to a

		social group.
		• Competence
		• Autonomy
		• Relatedness
		•
	Goal Orientation (Pintrich, Shunk)	• Mastery vs. performance
		• Feedback
	Weiner's Theory of Causal Attribution	Describes a person's view, explanations, justifications, and excuses on the influences of motivation for a task
		• Locus of control
		• Stability of the event
		• Controllability of the event
		Helps to explain the following reasons for success or failure
		• Low or high aptitude
		• Lack or preparedness of studies
		• Sickness on day of exam
		• Requirements are hard/easy
		• Instructor is fair or biased
		• Good luck or bad luck
		• Friends help or failed to help
Behavioral	Skinner	• Operant conditioning
		○ Conditioned responses
		○ Antecedents
		○ Consequences
		○ Reinforcement
		○ Punishment
		○ Applied behavior analysis
		○ Premack principle
		○ Response cost
		○ Contingency contracts and token reinforcement
	Jones	• Classroom structure to discourage misbehavior (rules, routines, room arrangement
		• Setting limits through body language (proximity, body carriage, facial expressions, eye contact)
		• Using Say, See, Do Teaching
Language Development	Sociocultural	• Vygotsky

Bilingual Education & Bilingualism	Baker, C	• Bilingual education in US
		• Immersion education
	Bernhardt, E.	• Acquisition of reading in second language students
		• Includes theoretical models of reading process, application to second language context
		• Curriculum, instruction and assessment
	Hornberger, N	• Biliteracy in an ecological framework
	Cummins, J	• Interactions between teachers and students
		• Understanding sociopolitical and psychological linguistic and

		pedagogical factors • Key structures and advocating
	Echevarria, J	• Model for sheltered instruction
	Geneva, G	• Culturally responsive teaching • Teacher caring, attitudes and expectations
	Handbook of Reading Research	• Comprehensive • Current methodology • Research based knowledge
	Herrera, S	• Differentiated instruction for linguistically diverse students • Includes transitional needs: cultural, academic, cognitive and linguistic
	Krashen, S	• Second language acquisition • Acquisition theory and application • Reading aloud, light reading, reading nontraditional forms of literature
	Nieto, S	• Cross-cultural and multilingual learning environments •
	National Reading Panel	• Comprehensive methodology and research: alphabetics, fluency, comprehension, teacher education and reading instruction, computer technology and reading

Made in the USA
Middletown, DE
17 August 2017